Babylon: The Gateway to the Gods

Anthony Fox

chipmunkapublishing
the mental health publisher

Anthony Fox

All rights reserved, no part of this publication may be reproduced by any means, electronic, mechanical photocopying, documentary, film or in any other format without prior written permission of the publisher.

>Published by
>Chipmunkapublishing
>United Kingdom

http://www.chipmunkapublishing.com

Copyright © Anthony Fox 2017

ISBN   978-1-78382-391-8

I thank family and friends for their encouragement during this project.

Anthony Fox

He was called Pharrell Anderson. The first time she met him they were both visiting Thailand, but they had different goals. It was a hot and humid day even though the heavens had just opened up with torrential rain, which lasted for several minutes, and then it just stopped as if it had never started; it was typical of that part of the world. The rainy season in Bangkok lasted for about three months from April until August, but for most of the time the sun was out in-between the bursts of rain, so life carried on much the same. Standing in front of the '*Shrine of Destiny*' where most tourists consider it to be older than it looks; she saw the first glimpse of him.

Pharrell was busy taking photos with his cell phone. His first few words to her were, "They call it the Shrine of Destiny" and then he spoke about his passion for books and why he felt the Shrine had significant importance to his quest. Pharrell's quest had brought him to the Far East, far from his home in search of a book, a very special book, a book that would make his name and fortune, he had explained to her.

In search of a book not just any book, but a piece of history that had been lost to the world of the antiquarian book collector for thousands of years. Like the Dead Sea Scrolls it was just waiting to be found. Perhaps, he had said it would be found in a cave or an excavated grave in some part of the middle-east somewhere. Pharrell told her that he was not like any other collector, and he was always searching for that rare, exceptionally rare find that no other collector had in their possession. The quest for him was more important; he had explained to her and that it added spice to his life. Approaching his mid-thirties he had never tired of the relentless search for that Golden

Chalice of finding that incredible rarity wherever in the world his quest would take him.

They continued in conversation in the shade of the giant wooden Buddha for several minutes, exchanging pleasantries and information about each other. They had immediately found each other attractive; she liked his Scandinavian good looks with his blond hair and steel blue eyes and the way he had confidently held a conversation, and for him it was her diminutive figure shaped like a guitar with auburn hair curling down to her shoulders and her seductive brown eyes. He said, "The Shrine of Destiny is where people come to seek their destiny." He had explained that the shrine held the answers to the questions you care to ask. The shrine was like a cathedral in size, but built entirely from wood and was still being built. He explained to her that he had spent most of the past summers searching European cities in dusty almost forgotten second-hand book shops. Sometimes, he explained that these establishments often offered the richest pickings, and he would sometimes make new contacts with antiquarian book collectors, his experience he had gained over the many years since leaving university and building a business trading in antiquarian books and documents, which stood in his favour. There was a mutual interest in each other's stories. Pharrell had continued talking while tourists milled around the giant wooden temple that had been built, apparently, without the use of a single nail, he had been told.

"And what brought you to Thailand?" he asked her.

She told Pharrell that she often travelled the world as a freelance journalist on commission and expenses. This was partly true. But she had a secret to keep.

"This time, I'm researching the Thai Royal family. My editor wants a story."

They continued talking, and later before they parted and went their separate ways for the day they had exchanged phone numbers and promised to meet later that week for a drink.

***

When Pharrell arrived in Thailand his quest had been to find the '*Shahbla el Allah*' and to make his name and fortune. The '*Book of God*' as many collectors called it was the last known book to survive from time of the ancient Sumer civilisation. Archaeological scholars suggest that Sumer was a region in Mesopotamia which is now part of southern Iraq, which was an ancient civilisation that started around 5500 to 4000 BC long before the great pyramids of Egypt. The words of the '*Shahbla el Allah*' were originally written in cuneiform on clay tablets by the Sumerians and then translated into Phoenician later by the merchant traders of the Mediterranean who traded with the Babylonians who came after the Sumerians around 2000 BC. The cuneiform language according to scholars was thought to be one of the earliest known written languages and was formed by making impressions in soft clay forming symbols and sounds using a stylist tool shaped like a triangle before firing the clay tablets in a kiln to harden. The '*Shahbla el Allah*' contained the words of God so say the Sumerian and later the Babylonian astrologers who were masters of reading the stars. The Babylonian civilisation which succeeded the Sumerian and Akkadian civilisations in the Mesopotamian region became known for its incredible developments in art, culture, and science. The great Ishtar Gate of Babylon with its blue glazed bricks and raised animal depictions was considered to be one of the seven great ancient wonders of the world. A reconstruction of the Ishtar

Gate now resides in a Berlin museum in Germany. Babylon was a city state, and often called the 'Gateway to the Gods' because it was said that the Babylonian astrologers could see into the future.

Pharrell had awaked that morning after a heavy night in the hotel bar feeling groggy after downing too many American drinks. He had a panchance for the unusual and had spent the previous night enjoying the pleasures of American cocktails. Listening to the many ghost stories some of the other residents had told that night around the bar. Pharrell had been too drunk to care about having scary dreams. That morning Pharrell was about to embark on another adventure and unsure where it would lead.

***

After several hours driving Pharrell was still feeling groggy from the previous night's drinking spree. He had time to think while he drove the 800 kilometres to *Kusamon*, a small village in the north-east region of Thailand close to the Mekong River. The roads were well signposted from Bangkok and surprisingly pothole free compared to some of the roads in Norway, he thought.

His mind lingered as he continued his journey on the surprise meeting he had had the previous day with the girl called Angelique at the *'Shrine of Destiny'*. He was curious about her and aroused at the prospect of meeting her again. Her long shapely legs at first glance had caught his eyes. Her coconut fair skin and auburn hair matched her deep brown eyes. The prospect of meeting her again stirred his loins as he made his way to Hugo's home. She was from America that was obvious from her accent, he surmised.

The phone call he had received from Hugo his friend the previous night had intrigued him. "Come here tomorrow, I will show you," he had said. "I can't tell you over the phone, they may be listening."

Who was listening and what he had to show Pharrell was a mystery he had to follow. It was part of his character to follow mysteries and go on adventures wherever it took him. All sorts of scenarios went through his mind, but he trusted his good friend for many years for finding rare antiquarian documents and books. They had first met at a book auction for collectors in Paris back in the 90's and they had become good friends and stayed in touch ever since. Pharrell was looking forward to seeing Hugo again; it had been several years since their paths had crossed even though they had kept in touch often over the phone. Hugo was a roly-poly of a man with a belly to match his Father Christmas silvery long beard, but he always had a keen eye and was no slouch when came to finding rare books. The French have panache for cooking and eating and Hugo was no exception when it came to good food and wine, he mused.

The directions Hugo had given Pharrell over the phone were precise. "Make sure no one follows you and get here before sunset," he had explained.

Pharrell consistently checked his rear view mirror and he had made sure no one was following him. For most of the journey the roads were deserted except from the occasional truck passing in the opposite direction. He had purposely set out early that morning realising the journey to Hugo's home would take many hours. All he could see ahead was vast tracks of farmland and in the distance the remote jungle that covered the mountain tops. The fields of flat rice paddies to the left and right of him were laid out in rectangles with the occasional tree offering shade to those who laboured in the fields.

The heat and humidity of the day started to cool as rain poured down making the journey a lot more tolerable. Pharrell was close to Hugo's home now he could see the mountains in the distance and parts of the river that Hugo had said often flooded the area in the rainy season. Pharrell turned off the main road and onto a dirt track, and followed its curious path for several minutes and finally he could see Hugo's home as he had described the previous night over the phone. The house was made of timber and built on stilts several feet above the ground to avoid the yearly floods. Pharrell noticed the house was encircled by palm, banana, and coconut trees. And, in the distance, he could see just miles of rice paddy fields and the sporadic roof tops of other homes scarcely piercing the horizon between the trees and the paddy fields.

As he parked the car and got out he noticed the faint smell of charcoal burning and wondered where it was coming from. Approaching the front steps to the house he called out and knocked on the door. He could hear the rustle of tiny footsteps, and, as the door opened, he saw the tiny shape of a woman. She had the features of a Thai girl with long graceful hair as dark as night with deep brown eyes with a diminutive slender body, and to him she looked about half Hugo's age. Pharrell felt surprised but intrigued, Hugo had not mentioned a word about a woman over the phone; but it made sense, who would want to live out here all alone miles from the nearest house, he said to himself?

"My name is Ning and you are Pharrell, yes," she said in broken English. "Please, come in, Hugo has been waiting for you to arrive."

Ning led Pharrell into a room that was almost dark with only the shards of light shining through between the venetian blinds hung at the windows, but it was enough for him to see. The noise of a whirling ceiling fan he felt as it cooled his face and kept the room cool from the heat and humidity from outside. It took a few seconds before his eyes adjusted to the darkness and it was then he was ushered by the girl to take a seat. It wasn't long before he could hear the thud of heavy footsteps and the voice of Hugo talking in French to Ning.

"*Mon cher ami*, how are you? Pleasant journey I hope," Hugo roared. Not waiting for a reply, he asked, "Listen were you followed?"

"No, I didn't see anyone. I was careful, Hugo," Pharrell replied.

"Why all the secrecy Hugo, what is so important that I had to drive for eight hours to see you?" Pharrell felt tired and hoped the journey to see his friend had been worthwhile, not just another goose chase orchestrated on some crazy idea.

"Do you remember the legend told about the richest king of Babylon?"

"Yes, continue Hugo," Pharrell said tediously, not wanting to disappoint Hugo who he knew liked to tell stories, even if sometimes the stories would drag on until his patience waned like the cycles of the moon.

Hugo had begun by explaining to Pharrell how the legend recalls why the king's treasure was never found. How a stranger one day arrived in the king's court. This stranger was not dressed like a court courtesan nor was he dressed like a beggar from the streets. This stranger so says the legend was a messenger from God. The messenger had told the king that his treasure was gone. The messenger then told the king that what you value in this life has no value in the next. The king and the messenger went to where the treasure was stored. In this stone strong room a former dungeon beneath the palace, which was guarded day and night all of the king's treasures from past conquests were stored. As the guards opened the door to the dungeon all they could see was dust and no shiny gold or jewels.

Pharrell roared with laughter and said, "Don't tell me you have found the treasure, Hugo." Pharrell had hoped Hugo would see the funny side of his comment.

"No, possibly more value than the treasure Pharrell. Let me finish," Hugo continued. Pharrell's eyes looked on with anticipation. He was beginning to find a renewed interest in what Hugo had to say. He had eyes for no one but the larger than life figure of Hugo.

Hugo continued to explain to Pharrell how the entire king's treasure from his previous conquests in his younger days from West of the Euphrates and East of the Niger was gone. The legend then says the king then asked the stranger where is my treasure and who are you? The stranger then said they call me the messenger of thy father. The legend then goes on to say that the stranger turned and walked away and disappeared as if he was never there. The legend then says the slaves of Babylon were set free and allowed to return to the land of milk and honey. The land they call Israel today. All this happened so the legend says, shortly after meeting the messenger and before the king died a few months later.

Hugo paused briefly to see the expression of his friend's face and then said, "Many people today believe that the king's treasure was the price the king paid to live a few extra months."

"Where does the legend come from?" Pharrell asked.

"That's the point Pharrell. Until now, nobody has had any idea how the legend was passed down the centuries, except from word of mouth. Most scholars of Babylonian antiquity have assumed that the legend was just a tale told to teach a moral and so the legend was passed from father to son and so on over the eons."

"Do you know how the alphabet was invented?" Hugo asked as if he was keen to impart some of his considerable knowledge to Pharrell.

"Yes, the Phoenicians invented the alphabet. They needed a written form of communication so they could trade and record their trading from port to port around the Mediterranean."

"Yes, that's right Pharrell. The Phoenicians who traded from port to port around the Mediterranean were the first to invent the alphabet, and then the Greeks improved it by adding a few extra characters."

Hugo was about to continue talking when the door suddenly opened and Ning entered the room carrying a tray with food and a bottle of wine. This presented Pharrell with a chance to admire the beauty of Ning, while she served the food and poured the wine. He could see why Hugo had settled down in Thailand. The Thai women like to please their men with a smile and more, he mused.

Hugo was always a good host. The bottle of *Pineau d'Anjou Vin* was a welcome distraction after the laborious journey, he thought.

"You have landed well…where did you meet Ning?" Pharrell asked curiously eager to learn more about this beautiful woman.

"We met down south…at the coast near *Chonburi*. She was working there in a tourist information office at the time. We got talking as you do, and I fell in love. She also speaks French which I found refreshing, and as you know not many people speak French here in Thailand."

"Anyway, you were saying about how the Greeks improved the alphabet," Pharrell interjected hoping his impatience had not been noticed by Hugo and Ning.

"Yes, it's the Greeks and the Phoenicians we have to thank for our present day alphabet. We should raise a glass of this fine wine and toast them because without them we may well be dealing with many more difficult characters and letters like the Mandarin the Chinese use," Hugo paused, raising a glass of wine to his lips.

"Cheers, *mon cher ami*."

"Pharrell, the reason why I asked if you were followed is because I believe I was followed the other day on the way here from Bangkok. A black Mercedes was on my tail for most of the journey. I could see the driver and passenger in my rear mirror they were both male. They made no attempt to overtake me…even when I purposely slowed down at different stages of the journey. I even pulled of the motorway to get gas to see what they would do."

"What did they do, Hugo?"

"Shortly after getting gas, and getting on the motorway again, I saw the black Mercedes back on my tail within a few minutes."

"Are you sure, Hugo?"

"Yes, definitely the same…," Hugo replied curtly before continuing. "I made a mental note of the license plate before I stopped for gas."

"It could have been tourists, and maybe you just got spooked out," Pharrell calmly said as he sipped some wine from his glass. He noticed Hugo's face had turned red and saw the sweat across his brow.

"Maybe, but the phone line here has been clicking…like someone is listening in. That has never happened before or at least I have never noticed it before."

"What happened to the Mercedes?"

"It turned off the main road a few kilometres from here," Hugo replied with a look of relief clearly visible on his face as if he was reliving the event in his mind.

"In this business you can't be too careful," Hugo stressed before he continued to explain the murky world of the antiquities market. Pharrell and Ning listened intently as they sat comfortably cooled by the swirling ceiling fan.

"There are always criminals willing to steal from me and you," he said as he continued to tell his story. Hugo explained that fakes and forgeries were passed off all the time in the antiquarian book and document market and that the Far East was a forger's paradise. He stressed that the Thai and Laos mafia were well known to be operating in this market because it's a lot easier to make serious money selling forgeries than it is to smuggle and sell drugs across borders.

"A couple of days ago, I had a phone call from a friend and dealer in antiques in Algeria. He's a Russian with contacts in Iraq," he said. Hugo then explained what he knew about the Russian. When the Americans in the Iraq war deposed of Saddam Hussein's government the country was ransacked and many precious artefacts stored in museums around the country were looted, especially, from the national museum in Baghdad. Some of these looted treasures found their way to collectors around the world via Algeria. Hugo explained how Algeria had become a haven for some of these artefacts. He stressed how easy it was to smuggle goods into Europe across the short sea crossing between Spain and Algeria.

"My Russian contact has offered his services many times before, which I have never used. I prefer to conduct my business legitimately, but many dealers and collectors are not so fussy."

"What's his name?" Pharrell asked curiously keen to learn more.

"Oleg Dimitrov," Hugo replied, as he took a big gulp of wine from his glass, before continuing his description of the Russian. "He is old school…from the days when Iraq was in bed with Russia. He's a big fat Russian, a former army trainer, who helped train Iraq's army, and then he retired. He then started a business dealing in antiques in Iraq before fleeing to Algeria when Saddam Hussein was deposed by the Americans."

Hugo paused and sipped some more wine from his glass before continuing, "Oleg sent me an email with a copy of a Greek papyrus which seems to confirm the story about the richest king of Babylon. He's offering it for sale. I have printed the email. Here take a look and tell me what you think?"

"My Greek is not up to translating this Hugo, besides this is old Greek and part Aramaic, which was how they spoke in the time before and after Jesus Christ," Pharrell replied.

"Sorry, Pharrell…read this other document. I have translated the document the best I can into English. In the meantime, I have forwarded the original email to a Paris academic, who is a professor of antiquities at the University of Paris to get a comprehensive translation, and I'm waiting for her reply. Her name is Lucy Bouchard, she is an old friend from my younger days when I was a student living the bohemian life in Paris." This brought a gleaming broad smile across Hugo's face as he relived his youth for short time.

Pharrell began reading the document slowly and carefully, occasionally, stopping only to look at his friend briefly while his friend continued to talk. Hugo's enthusiasm was clearly demonstrated in his voice and body language. He was like a child playing with a new toy you could not stop his imagination and zeal overshadowing everything else.

"The document mentions the richest king of Babylon as King Nebuchadnezzar. The same king, who ransacked Jerusalem and destroyed the first temple, built by Solomon, and who then exiled the Jews who survived to the kingdom of Babylon," said Hugo emphasising the importance of King Nebuchadnezzar in history to Pharrell.

"But wasn't it King Cyrus that freed the Jews?"

Pharrell explained that the legend of the richest king of Babylon had always been associated with King Cyrus II also known as 'Cyrus the Great' by scholars, but never proved. The great achievements in art, culture, and science during the reign of King Nebuchadnezzar who built the great Ishtar Gate at the walls of the city of Babylon was according to many scholars the king associated with the legend of the richest king of Babylon. After the fall and conquest of Jerusalem in 587 BC by the Babylonians the Jews that survived were forcibly marched into captivity by King Nebuchadnezzar and taken to Babylon. It would be several generations before King Cyrus II conquered the empire of the Babylonians in around 537 BC and close to a year later that Cyrus the Great made a proclamation and freed the Jews in captivity in Babylon. It was then that Cyrus the Great encouraged the Jews to rebuild the Temple of Solomon previously destroyed by Nebuchadnezzar. It was said that Cyrus the Great, after his conquest of Babylon, claimed to be not only king of

Babylon, Sumer and Akkad, but king of the *'four corners of the world'*. It was according to scholars the largest empire the world had ever seen. Cyrus was the founder of the Persian Empire that according to scholars lasted about two hundred years before Alexander the Great the king of Macedonia defeated the last king of Persia Darius II at the battle of Gaugamela, east of modern Mosul in Iraq.

"Yes, you are right, but perhaps the legend started with Nebuchadnezzar and finished with Cyrus the Great. You know how legends over time get expanded," said Hugo, trying to convince his friend. "Possibly, this is the proof."

"Proof of what, the treasure?" retorted Pharrell. "Don't get ahead of yourself Hugo. Scholars will want to pour over this Greek papyrus for years before they believe its authenticity," continued Pharrell, wanting to cool Hugo's undoubted enthusiasm before it got out of control.

"Yes, I know, but it could be genuine and if it is the market for this will be wide open with buyers from around the world willing to pay top dollar. Especially, the Americans, their museums and collectors have to have everything of rarity, you should know that Pharrell," Hugo replied brusquely to Pharrell's previous comments unwilling to dampen his new found enthusiasm.

Pharrell continued reading Hugo's translation, while Hugo mused over another glass of wine. His friend, occasionally, was sipping wine while he continued to talk about Oleg and how they first met. Most of which, Pharrell did not take in, as he was busy trying to read the document and was not listening to what Hugo had to say about his Russian friend.

As Pharrell read the words...*the prophecy of Babylon shall be forever*...he remembered that the Holy Bible describes a prophecy about Babylon, the so-called Babylonian mystery.

"What do you think?" Hugo asked eager to know the thoughts of Pharrell before he had finished reading the document.

Pharrell's eyes glanced at Hugo and with a nod of agreement spoke briefly before returning to read the rest of the document.

As Pharrell finished reading the document he enquired, "I would like to see the full translation...before I make up my mind. But, it's a very interesting document if it turns out to be genuine. Where do I figure in this?"

Hugo replied, "I should hear from Lucy Bouchard within a few days at the latest. I asked her to get back to me as soon as possible...she knows it's urgent, I stressed that point in the email. I will phone her later today. Just to make sure she has received the email."

"Oh, what has this to do with me, Hugo? Where do I figure in this mystery?" Pharrell inquired again.

"I want you to accompany me to Algeria to see Oleg. I need your expertise when dealing with the Russian. Besides, it's safer with the two of us strolling around the back streets of Algeria in that part of the world then on my own. There are so many beggars and thieves there that they will prey on tourists on their own. I will pay all expenses and if this papyrus turns out to be genuine we will split the profit eighty percent for me and twenty percent for you. How does that sound?"

Pharrell queried, "How long would we be there for?"

"Only a couple of days at most, I suspect."

"Okay, Hugo, let's do it, it's a deal."

Both men briefly shook hands across the coffee table and then raised their glasses in the air to toast the deal.

The light in the room had begun to fade as the day had begun its journey into early evening.

"You can stay the night Pharrell if you don't fancy the journey back to Bangkok…we have a spare bed. It's up to you; we can catch up on old times. And Ning is a great cook…she will enjoy feeding us. She has a speciality dish called *Khao Na Pet,* which she likes to cook."

"Thanks for the offer…I will take you up on that. I don't like driving at night, especially, in Thailand some of the locals don't always drive on the correct side of the road at the best of times." They all laughed including Ning.

"Great, Ning will want to pop down to the local market before it gets too dark."

As Hugo and Ning proceeded to leave the room Pharrell's mind drifted momentarily back to the meeting he had the other day with the girl at the *'Shrine of Destiny'*. He was thinking, how her shapely body had caught his attention. It had been a long time since his last romantic interlude. Too long, he said to himself.

***

The journey back to Bangkok for Pharrell was uneventful apart from the hurried stop at a rest area he had to make. Most of toilets were for the locals and not designed for westerners to bend down to; luckily he found one just in time designed for foreigners. The previous night's food of roast duck on a bed of rice was tasty and indeed Ning was a good cook but, his stomach was not used to rich spices combined with too much wine. He had an aversion to rich food and had been this way since a young boy growing up in Stavanger, Norway.

On the journey back to Bangkok Pharrell had time to think…*the prophecy of Babylon shall be forever*…the words he had read on the document resonated in his mind. Why does the so-called Babylonian mystery still puzzle scholars today, it was a mystery that he needed to solve if possible?

***

The next day, Pharrell had arranged to meet Angelique the girl he had met at the *'Shrine of Destiny'* the other day. They had decided to meet at noon, at a bar, she had recommended near the Hilton hotel at the centre of the financial district in Bangkok. He brought with him a copy of the papyrus and a copy of Hugo's translation for her perusal.

From where he sat, he could observe the streets. Tourists mingled with smartly dressed business people along the crowded pavements. A young couple sat on a bench at the bus stop were kissing while the Bangkok traffic slowly passed them by. The street vendors were busy with people buying their wares. Most people seemed to be buying food and drinks to refresh and cool them from the heat of the day.

He felt the choking heat of Bangkok and the pungent fumes of the traffic clogging his throat. He realised then why Hugo preferred the north of Thailand, it was cooler there and he could breathe clean air. Perhaps, one day he would live in a similar place away from the maddening crowds and pollution, he said to himself.

"Would you like a drink, sir?" the waiter asked.

He ordered a drink and patiently waited the arrival of Angelique. His thoughts were of the girl he had met at the *'Shrine of Destiny'* and of Hugo, who had rekindled his sense of adventure. The documents he had brought with him to show Angelique were just talking pieces and nothing more, he was thinking.

"That Hugo...," he said to himself, without completing the thought. The day was getting hotter, and he felt a trickle of sweat roll down his face onto to his hand. Pharrell felt jealous of the couple at the bus stop, and saw that he could have the same passion with a woman. There was nothing holding him back except himself. The quest of finding the *Shahbla el Allah*, the trip to Algeria, and the desire to explore were all part of his character, it was his destiny, he said to himself.

Most men approaching their mid-thirties are married with children, and settled down with a mortgage and not chasing a dream of fame and fortune from one country to another. The same goes for women in their mid-thirties, and typically all the pretty ones are already married, he laughed at himself as these thoughts resonated in his mind.

"Would you like something more?" the waiter asked, placing the drink on the table.

"Yes, same again...coke and Jack Daniels with ice." Pharrell felt the need to quench his dry mouth before Angelique arrived. The hot air and humidity had got to him, but he sensed in the air that there would be rain before the day turned to night, but he was thankful for the light breeze that helped cool his body and stem the treacle of sweat from the top of his head.

The French have a passion for their wine and he had a taste for liquor, he mused. Hugo certainly had a passion for food and wine that was clearly visible by his portly size. Perhaps, someday he was due the same outcome as Hugo. To retire to some backwater and live with a beautiful woman while indulging in good food and wine seemed like an enviable prospect.

From where he was seated he saw Angelique wave her hand. Coming towards the bar he saw her finely tuned body as the sun's rays shone through her dress providing a glimpse of her silhouette. He stood up to greet her. Allowing him to glimpse more of her shapely silhouette through her dress the closer she came.

"Hello Pharrell…sorry I'm late," she said greeting him with a smile and with a brief peck to both his cheeks.

"It's okay…what would you like to drink?" he said as he gestured with the palms of his hands to Angelique to take a seat.

"Whatever you are having…that's fine for me. Did you have any trouble finding the bar?"

Pharrell saw the waiter approaching and ordered some more drinks before taking his seat again. He felt relaxed and happy at the sight of Angelique. It had been a long time that he had the pleasure of the company of a beautiful woman. It was almost like a new experience, it had been so long since he felt aroused.

"No problem, your directions made it easy," Pharrell replied smiling hoping his nervousness inside would soon disappear. "Have you had a good week, so far?" he inquired.

"Yes…been busy researching the Royal family. I have also interviewed some important people in the Thai government. And I have started to draft a story for my editor."

"Have you been busy Pharrell?" she asked.

Reaching into his pocket he pulled out the documents he had wanted to show her. He carefully unfolded the paper copies he had brought back from Hugo's home. Unfolding the paper copies he saw Angelique's eyes follow his every move.

"What's this?" she asked curiously.

"It's a copy of an old Greek papyrus document and a copy of the translation my friend Hugo made. Remember, I briefly told you about Hugo on the phone last night. Tell me what you think?"

Pharrell quenched his dry throat with a mouthful of his drink, as Angelique inquisitively examined the documents. He felt more sweat roll down his face. From where he sat, he could observe her every move. He saw the wind gently caress her hair. He sensed the warmness in his loins.

"It sounds intriguing…what does the prophecy of Babylon mean?" she asked.

"It comes from the Bible…from the book of Jeramiah and Isaiah. The prophecy says that Babylon to be cut off, that none shall remain in it; neither man nor animal shall live there forever more. Today, Babylon is uninhabited and has been since before Jesus Christ. The prophets Jeramiah and Isaiah prophesied about the destruction of Babylon hundreds of years before the event. Today, it's mostly a pile of bricks and sand apart from what has been excavated and rebuilt for the tourists. But, since the Iraq war the whole country is in turmoil and very few tourists would want to go there today."

"The document also mentions King Nebuchadnezzar. I remember reading in the Bible about King Nebuchadnezzar as a child. He captured and destroyed the city of Jerusalem and enslaved the Jews into captivity and then transported them back to the city of Babylon," she said.

"Yes, that is correct," Pharrell responded.

"How is this related to your quest? The quest you told me about the day we first met at the '*Shrine of Destiny*'," she curiously asked.

"It doesn't directly."

"But, remember I told you I was searching for clues to the so-called *Shahbla el Allah*. Well, Babylon is often referred to as the *'City of God'* or the *'Gateway to the Gods'* and perhaps this papyrus will provide more clues if it's genuine. Hugo sent a copy of the papyrus for a translation to an academic in Paris who is an expert in ancient Greek and Aramaic. Within a day or two we shall have the full translation to digest."

"What will you do then?" Angelique enquired.

"Hugo and I are planning a trip to Algeria to see the dealer who wants to sell the original papyrus. Hugo needs my expertise and experience dealing in old manuscripts; he also feels it's safer together on the streets of Algeria than on his own."

"So…you are leaving me, so soon. When will you leave?" she asked with a cute smile.

"In a few days…but, I will be back here before you have time to miss me," he replied with a cheeky chuckle. Pharrell could sense a deeper friendship developing and he hoped for more. Perhaps, she also felt the same closeness, he mused.

They continued talking and exchanging information about each other. They ordered some more drinks and some food. Pharrell sensed a mutual interest in each other's stories. He saw the colour of her face redden from the compliments he gave her. He felt the wind getting stronger cooling his face and body more and more. And he perceived that the afternoon rain was imminent.

"I think it's going to rain…its cooler now and the clouds have darkened. Perhaps we should find a table inside before the Bangkok monsoon starts."

"Are you psychic?" she challenged him.

"Sometimes, since a child growing up in Stavanger I have relied on my intuition to guide me. Let me see, where is my crystal ball, perhaps, I can read your future." he replied cheekily, as they both laughed at his comments.

Pharrell explained that since a young boy growing up in Stavanger in Norway the winters were cold, bitter and harsh and he would while away the long dark days and nights reading as much as he could. His deep blue eyes would glisten at the prospect of finding second-hand books in shops around the back streets of the city. His parents were antique dealers and often second-hand books came into their possession during the course of their business. He would read these books as it did not cost him any of his limited pocket money funds to acquire.

Throughout Pharrell's childhood he had spent many hours dreaming of the quests he would follow as a man. He enjoyed listening to the stories his grandfather would tell that inspired his love of adventure and he promised himself that one day he would also be an adventurer. His grandfather had taught him to love books because he would often say, 'Treasure knowledge more than wealth' and you will never be poor because wisdom and truth are often hidden within books. His grandfather had inspired his imagination, and he had never looked back since. His love of books was the spaceships in his mind of where in the world he would travel to the future. The allure of the far-east, the mysteries of the jungles of Africa and other far-flung forgotten places of history inspired his mind during the endless dreary winters of Stavanger and the school time that he never did like.

"I remember, I was only twelve or thirteen years old going to school one day, and I had a strange feeling something bad was going to happen. All day, I had the same feeling. And when I got home from school my mother and father were there to greet me. Normally, they would be at work at that time of day. So, immediately I saw them, I realised something was wrong. My grandfather had died that morning," Pharrell said near to tears.

"I was upset and cried all night. I loved my grandparents. My grandfather taught me a lot about life, he always had time for me."

At that moment Angelique saw Pharrell wipe a tear from his eye. She felt closer to him now. She understood his loss; she also had lost siblings she loved. She felt the emotion as tears began to fall from her eyes. She tried to stop the tears by rubbing her eyes dry until the tears abated.

"Shall we find a table inside?" he asked again. He thought it best to change the conversation before his emotions let loose.

"No, I have to go back to my hotel soon. I'm expecting a call from Henry my editor. He always phones me early evening Bangkok time for a brief on the story I'm writing. It's the only mutually convenient time for both of us, because New York is about eleven hours behind of Bangkok time," she replied.

"Tell me, what was your grandfather like?"

"He told me when he was young, he sailed the seas working as a merchant seaman and worked his way up the ladder to captain. He liked the freedom of sailing the oceans from port to port. I guess, I have inherited his spirit of adventure," Pharrell replied.

Before answering, she glanced at her watch. "It seems so." She saw the first spots of rain hit the ground. She felt the dampness of the wind provide relief from the heat as it cooled her body.

"I better go before the downpour starts. Ring me tomorrow."

They said their goodbyes with an embrace. Pharrell promised he would phone her before watching her disappear into the melee of the Bangkok crowds busy trying to avoid the impending Monsoon rain.

***

"Hello, *mon cher ami*. Can you hear me?" Hugo said, over the noisy crackle on the phone line.

"Yes, I can hear you Hugo, but the connection keeps fading," Pharrell replied, raising his voice loud enough above the crackling sound of the telephone connection to be heard at the other end and most likely into the bedrooms either side of his in the hotel.

"I have sent you an email with the full translation of the papyrus manuscript that I received from Lucy Bouchard late last night. Have you received the email?" Hugo asked keenly.

"Yes, I have the email you sent," Pharrell replied.

"Lucy seems convinced the document is genuine, her opinion is based on the use of language structure from that period. She thinks any forger would have to be an expert on ancient Greek and Aramaic combined with an expertise in language structure for that era. I spoke with the dealer in Algeria this morning and I told him I would be there in a couple of days. I have made reservations for the flight for tomorrow evening that way we will arrive in Algeria the following morning," Hugo explained.

"What was that you said, Hugo," Pharrell asked, as the phone connection faded again.

"Never mind, it's all in the email. Are you ready to go?"

"Yes, been waiting since we decided to go to Algeria," Pharrell bellowed.

"Okay, speak to you tomorrow…cheers," Hugo said, as the noisy crackle of the phone stopped.

Pharrell heard the sound of the mobile phone connection end. The mobile phone system in Thailand was erratic at the best of times, especially, in the remote parts of the country. Where Hugo was living, in the North East of Thailand close to the Mekong River and the border with Laos, he surmised that it was probably the reason why the mobile's connection signal kept fading. Hugo must have used a mobile instead of his landline connection, which he felt was being listened into.

***

As Hugo and Pharrell disembarked from the plane onto the tarmac they felt the morning air of Algeria as sweat slowly trickled down their faces. The heat was different from Thailand; the air was bone dry and the wind from the desert brought clouds of desert dust and sand. They could taste the sand as they tried to avoid the gusts of wind blowing sand into their eyes. Hugo held his Panama hat down with one hand while avoiding the dust clouds from obscuring his vision as they walked the short distance to the airport terminal. Pharrell felt his shirt cling to his skin as more and more sweat rolled down his back. As he walked with the other passengers to the terminal he observed the Arabs. He saw that most of the Arab women were dressed in the traditional black *Hijab* dress with most of their body covered from head to toe, with only there face on show. Although, some of the woman were completely concealed except for their eyes as they were wearing the traditional *Niqab* dress. He noticed the men whom he assumed were Arab from their facial features with their dark skin and jet black hair wore mostly western cloths and they showed no signs that the heat bothered them.

Hugo and Pharrell appreciated the air conditioning of the airport terminal building away from the stifling heat and the dusty wind outside. Their progress through passport control and customs was uneventful for them; although they saw a crowd of security men and women some with side arms and machine guns surround one unfortunate soul. They recognized the passenger was from their flight, an American boy. They had overheard the teenager talking with another passenger on the plane that he was from Milwaukee, and that he was travelling to Algeria to visit a friend who worked in the oil industry.

Pharrell imagined that the Arabs treated Americans differently compared to other foreigners because of the Palestinian Israeli conflict, he was thinking. Perhaps, he was making too many assumptions, but there was probably some truth in his thinking, he said to himself while he waited to go through passport control.

On the way to the hotel from the airport they observed the hustle and bustle of daily life from the back seat of the taxi. They saw the hawkers on the streets of Algiers selling just about everything from food to trinkets to the tourists. They could see how the Arab women, dressed in their black traditional dress stood out from the tourists in their brightly coloured clothes with their sunglasses and cameras. The day was getting hotter they could feel the hot air from outside rush in through the open windows of the taxi. The sun's rays burned their backs through the back window as sweat rolled down their faces. Without the luxury of air conditioning in the 1980's Ford Saloon they were travelling in they felt the dust and heat choke their throats as the taxi made its way through the city traffic of Algiers. As the taxi stopped at a major traffic inter section a woman carrying a baby approached them, she spoke in broken English and gestured for money. They saw how the dirt and dust from the pollution of the cars had covered her clothes and face. The taxi driver spoke in Arabic to her and gestured with his hand in anger at her to go away. Pharrell took pity on her and reached out and gave her some money and she thanked him before moving to the next vehicle in the queue. The taxi driver mumbled something in Arabic to Pharrell and he could see his displeasure in the driver's face through the rear view mirror as they continued their journey to the hotel.

When they finally reached the hotel they could see the building was recently constructed and contemporary to western hotels, and as they walked in inside there was relief from the heat outside as the hotel's ceiling fans whirled, cooling them as they waited in the reception area. At least Hugo had booked a modern hotel for their stay, Pharrell said to himself.

After checking in and watching the scurry of the hotel's porters eager to collect the few items of luggage they had brought for a two day stay they were shown their room. Their room was on the tenth floor with two double beds and a balcony with a vista of the city. Pharrell realised, why there was such a flurry by the porters to collect their luggage as they waited for a tip. He noticed it wasn't different to any other hotel in the world.

Within minutes Hugo was using the hotel's bedroom phone and arranging an outside call, while Pharrell showered and shaved. Pharrell could hear Hugo talking on the phone from the bathroom.

"We are staying at the Palace Appart Hotel room one hundred and nine." There was several minutes silence before he heard Hugo again. "Okay, see you at three at your premises," he said, as Pharrell then heard Hugo call out from the bedroom.

"Pharrell, I've made arrangements with the Russian, to meet at his place at three this afternoon. As soon as I've had a shower and change we can get something to eat."

"Sounds good, Hugo," Pharrell muttered.

As Pharrell waited for Hugo he could observe the sprawling city from the balcony. From where he sat he could hear the faint sounds of the traffic below and in the distance could see the familiar shape of an Islamic mosque, the dome's silhouette majestically forming a vista amongst the skyline of office blocks and other assorted buildings. And from a distance could hear the faint sounds of an Arabic voice calling the devoted to pray. He could also taste and smell the scent of pollution in the air from the city traffic far below.

***

As the taxi snaked its way around the narrow back streets of the city they passed the many bazaars and cafés where the locals spent their afternoons avoiding the sun and the tourists. Hugo and Pharrell could observe the men and women relaxing in the cafés with their Hookahs. The scent of the Hookahs burning their sweet smelling aromas on every street was in the air and soon filled the taxi as it turned each corner and slowly made its way to the Russian's premises.

"This is it," said Hugo.

From the outside, the building had seen better days. Thick dust and dirt had collated around the window frames and the dirt on the window glass obscured the view inside the shop. The door to the building had a sign saying, *closed*. Hugo knocked loudly on the door

and they waited a few minutes before they heard the sound of someone unlocking the door.
As the door opened, a middle-age Arab man greeted them with a smile, although most of his teeth were a mixture of black and gold.
"We have come to see Oleg," Hugo announced.
"Oh..., yes, my master told me," the Arab replied in broken English with a mix of an accent that almost sounded like he had had a public school education.
"Please...come in," the Arab said, as Pharrell and Hugo entered the dimly lit shop. Before they could ask where his master was the Arab was imparting the message.
"My master had to go out...and will be back soon," the Arab said, as Pharrell and Hugo looked at each other in surprise.
"I will bring you some coffee...please follow me," the Arab servant said, as he bowed and gestured with his hands to follow.
As Hugo and Pharrell sat where the Arab had gestured on a large well-worn leather couch and waited for the Russian to arrive they could observe the array of antiques for sale. The shop was full of Middle Eastern furniture, objects de art, paintings and fine Persia rugs. There was an Egyptian mummy staring at them from the corner of the room and a large marble statue of a Sphinx the size of a lion.
Moments later, the Arab servant appeared with a tray of fine Algerian black coffee and served in small delicate porcelain cups with no handles.
"Would you like to see our courtyard?" the Arab servant asked.
Hugo and Pharrell both nodded their heads in agreement and followed the Arab servant past the antique furniture and an Egyptian mummy to the back of the shop and into an enclosed open air courtyard.

"Sit here…I will bring your coffee."
Hugo and Pharrell noticed the courtyard was square in shape, and that it must provide light and fresh air to many of the rooms in the double floor building. The courtyard was full of colourful flowers with a Juniper tree in one corner providing shade from the sun and they could smell a sweet aroma from the purple petals as they sat under the tree drinking their coffee.
"At least we found the place without getting lost," Hugo announced with a chuckle in his voice. "The directions Oleg gave me for the taxi made it easy."
They were in an area of Algiers they call the 'Casbah of Algiers' famous for its narrow streets and old world buildings frequented by tourists during the day and at night by those seeking to smoke the hashish.
Pharrell just nodded with agreement, while he thought about the phone call with Angelique the day before. She had told him about a girlfriend who had been robbed at knife point while holidaying in Algeria. When the girl went to the local police to report the incident, the police had said she was foolish to be walking alone. Angelique had told him to be careful in Algeria. Those were her last words before saying goodbye. She was starting to care and perhaps starting to love him, the feeling was mutual, he thought. The thoughts of Angelique started to stimulate his emotions. He felt his loins stir and had to adjust his trousers for comfort and without Hugo catching sight of his predicament.
It was over an hour, before Oleg came into the courtyard announcing his arrival with orders to his servant to bring more fresh coffee for everyone. Hugo was right, Oleg was a giant with a loud voice to match his physique, Pharrell observed.
"*Skol'ko let, skol'ko zim!*" Oleg bellowed in Russian.

"Welcome Hugo, and who is this?" Oleg asked in English, while peering straight at Pharrell with his steel blue eyes. At the same time he had a grin on his face as if he owned the world.

"Oleg, this is my good friend Pharrell, who is assisting me with the possible purchase of the papyri you have for sale." Pharrell immediately felt the tremendous squeeze of his large hand as he shook hands with the giant Russian. Pharrell noticed the Russian looked more like a heavyweight boxer with huge muscular arms and a neck thicker than most people's legs carrying a bald head that was well tanned.

"You never mentioned on the phone you were bringing support with you...Hugo," Oleg said laughing, but there was seriousness clearly audible in the tone of his voice. And, his dark blue eyes peered straight at Hugo. "I understand. You don't trust me...hey?"

"No, it's not like that...Pharrell is an expert in old manuscripts and two heads are better than one," Hugo replied, his face blushing at the challenging question from the Russian.

"*Ya ponimaju.* Okay...Okay, I understand," Oleg muttered.

The Arab servant came into the courtyard carrying a tray of fresh coffee and some food. Then Oleg spoke some words in Russian to the Arab. And then the servant scurried off in a hurry as if he had been reprimanded for something, Pharrell surmised.

"*Za zdarov'e!*" Oleg announced in Russian and repeated in English the words, "Good health!"

Hugo and Pharrell waited for Oleg to start eating as the steam from the hot food filled the air with an aromatic smell that tempted their taste buds even though they were not hungry.

"Drink and eat. You should like this food. It is called *Golubtsy*, its ground beef mixed with boiled rice and spices wrapped in red cabbage leaves, it's one of the food dishes I have sent here from Russia each month, and it costs me a fortune. I much prefer my own country's food rather than the Algerian cuisine. They eat a lot of *Couscous* here and not much else," Oleg said with a mouthful of food undigested slurring his words.

"Finally…we can talk business," Oleg announced, as the Arab servant appeared holding a small wooden box that he presented to his master before bowing, and leaving the courtyard.

"These are Havana cigars, only the best you can buy," he chuckled with joy in his voice, while gesturing with his hand to Hugo and Pharrell to try one. Hugo and Pharrell felt obliged to try one as Oleg used the cigar cutter and lit his before offering the cutter and lighter to Hugo and Pharrell to use.

As Oleg inhaled and exhaled the cigar smoke with just a brief pause to issue some orders in Arabic to his servant, who then bowed and scampered away into one of the many doorways leading off from the courtyard.

"I have told my servant to bring the papyri," Oleg said.

Hugo and Pharrell could see the enjoyment in Oleg's face that the cigar gave him as he sat there relishing every puff like an artist purveying his work with satisfaction and elation. The courtyard was soon filled with the aroma of cigar smoke as all three of them waited for the servant to reappear with the papyri.

"I acquired a taste for these Havana's in my youth when I was in the Russian army and stationed in Cuba during the Cold War. These cigars are handmade, the women in Cuba roll the tobacco leaves on their thighs…I can almost taste their bodies as I smoke these," he said smiling and eyeing Pharrell's expression. Pharrell nodded his head with agreement and grinned back at Oleg with pleasure. Pharrell noticed the same pleasure on the face of Hugo. There was just silence between them as they all relished the cigars and relaxed under the Juniper tree.

"How long were you stationed in Cuba...Oleg?" Hugo asked.

"Nearly five years helping to train the Cuban army...had a great time. The women there are very beautiful and pleasing," Oleg replied, his face grinning like a Cheshire cat. For a moment, Oleg was about to tell a story, but instead, he just smiled and continued to enjoy his cigar.

Briefly, Pharrell thoughts were of Angelique and her shapely body as he sat and waited for the papyri to arrive. The pleasing thoughts and the relaxation of smoking the cigar had stirred his body and emotions. For him, it had been a long time, since he had had such thoughts. Hopefully, his companions had not noticed his adjustment of his trousers, he mused.

"Aarrhh, here is the papyri," Oleg murmured, as the servant handed a leather folder to him before bowing and leaving the courtyard. Oleg opened the folder and passed it towards Hugo and Pharrell for inspection. Hugo reached into his trouser back pocket and unfolded the paper copy of the papyri manuscript original sent via email to him by Oleg, and he also unfolded a copy of the translation prepared by Lucy Bouchard in Paris. Hugo felt the need to check he was dealing with the same papyri Oleg wanted to sell. Hugo and Pharrell carefully inspected the papyri. The papyri consisted of four separate sheets of papyrus with each papyrus enclosed in a plastic see through folder. Trusting on all their experience they cautiously examined the manuscript for some time, even smelling the papyri to sense its age while Oleg puffed away on his cigar with much enjoyment while eyeing their every move. At the same time Pharrell kept one eye on Oleg to see if Oleg's body language revealed a clue to any betrayal.

"Gentlemen...I have to make a phone call, please excuse me. You have time to discuss the papyri in private. Would you like some more coffee?" Oleg asked before making his way from the courtyard into the shop. Both Hugo and Pharrell declined the offer of more coffee as they were too busy examining the papyri.

"What's your analysis of the papyri, Pharrell?" Hugo asked intently but with such eagerness to know his friend's thoughts that he was like a psychic examining a crystal ball wanting to know someone's future.

"My gut feeling is...it has an age. It's difficult to fake several thousands of years. The condition also tells its own story...again difficult to fake. It also smells right...what I mean is, I could not smell any sign of chemicals. Also, from what Lucy said about the language structure used, it has a belonging from that era...that would also be difficult to fake. So far it looks genuine, the real test would be to analyse a fragment for carbon dating, but that would take possibly several weeks before we got the result, and we would have to rely on Oleg agreeing to the test," Pharrell replied.

"I agree with your assessment, it looks genuine and I have known Oleg for many years and I trust him. Furthermore, Oleg has a reputation in this business to honour...besides, if it was a fake it's not of his making," Hugo said.

"Yes...I understand, but money can do strange things to people, especially, when it involves large sums of money," Pharrell said interrupting Hugo's thoughts on his Russian friend's trustworthiness.

"Yes, I know," snapped Hugo. "But, I have known Oleg to be fair and honest…and like I said, I trust him."

"What will you do, Hugo?" Hugo paused momentarily with his eyes focused on the papyri, and with one hand under his nose, and the other playing with his silver beard in deep deliberation before answering. "Depends on what he is asking for the papyri, and on what terms."

"Let's hope it's reasonable and Oleg is willing to make terms," Pharrell said, while inhaling the cigar smoke. Pharrell felt dizzy from the cigar and remarked to Hugo the cigar tasted good and could see how Oleg had become addicted to their charm. Hugo nodded with agreement, but Pharrell could see that Hugo was not really listening, but he was in a kind of trance contemplating his next move. He noticed the appearance of sweat on his forehead as he puffed on his cigar waiting for Oleg to reappear.

Moments later, Oleg reappeared with a grin on his face and a fresh cigar in his hand. "Neeploha!" he roared. Hugo and Pharrell were unsure what this meant, but they both noticed how happy he looked.

"What do you say, Hugo?" Oleg asked.

"What price do you have in mind…*mon cher ami*?" Hugo enquired.

"Two hundred and fifty thousand dollars," Oleg answered with a tone of voice full of confidence and said nothing else. He had the experience of a seasoned salesman and knew all the tricks of the trade, and from the many years trading in antiques it had taught him that silence was like finding gold.

"That's a lot of money…for something that is not proven to be genuine," Hugo responded waiting to see the reaction of the Russian's face.

The Russia lit his cigar and sat there inhaling and exhaling the smoke and said nothing for what seemed several minutes, his facial expression revealing no clues. He peered at Hugo and Pharrell and took a deep breath and said, "Okay…I understand my friend, but before you make your decision to buy or not…I should tell you I have another dealer interested in the papyri."

Hugo had anticipated the negotiations would be tough. He felt the perspiration on his forehead start to treacle down his face. He noticed there was now more cigar smoke in the air masking the sweet smelling aroma of the Juniper tree. Clouds of smoke hung like circular spaceships all around their table. At times, his view of the Russian's face was blurred by the cigar smoke. He considered the possibility of another dealer's interest in buying the papyri could be true or a ploy, he said to himself.

"Can I take a fragment of the papyri for carbon dating?" Hugo asked sheepishly hoping the question would reveal a clue to the genuineness of the papyri, he thought.

"Yes…but you know and I know that it can take weeks before you get the results of the carbon dating. In the meantime, I can sell to someone else," Oleg replied curtly, as Hugo and Pharrell then noticed a wry smile between the puffs of the cigar smoke bellowing from the mouth of the Russian as he waited for an answer. To Hugo and Pharrell, the Russian looked like a man in control and happy with the negotiations, so far.

Hugo shook his head in agreement and said, "Okay, let's discuss terms first."

"What terms do you want?" Oleg asked.

"We are friends…right?"

"Yes, we are…but this is business, Hugo."

"I will pay you half now…and half when the carbon dating results prove it's genuine. Do we have a deal?" Hugo asked.

Without waiting for a reply, Hugo then said, "This way we both take a risk, but I'm taking the bigger risk." Hugo hoped his offer would seal the deal.

After several moments of silence, the Russian took several puffs of his cigar and nodded his head in agreement and then said, "Okay, we have a deal. Let's have a drink to celebrate."

Oleg shouted, "Yousef…Yousef." Moments later, the servant came scurrying into the courtyard and the Russian bellowed his instructions, "Bring glasses and the Vodka. But, first return this to its place," he said, as he placed the leather binder containing the papyri in the servant's outstretched hands.

Moments later, Yousef reappeared carrying a tray of glasses and a bottle of Russian Vodka to their table and then he scurried away into the shade of the building again like a mouse fleeing the presence of a cat. "*Na zdorovje*," Oleg roared in Russian as he poured the liquid to the brim of each glass, and then started gesturing with his hand for Hugo and Pharrell to toast the deal with him. "*Na zdorovje*," they all shouted as they all raised their glasses in the air.

Oleg then handed over his bank details to Hugo, who then promised the money, would be in his bank account within twenty four hours. "When I have received the money in my bank account…you can collect the papyri," Oleg retorted with a face now blushing red from the vodka and a smile bursting with confidence.

"The money should be in your account tomorrow. So, as soon as I receive confirmation from my bank that the transfer is complete then we shall contact you and pick up the papyri…is that okay with you, Oleg?" Hugo asked.

"Yes…fine, that is good," the Russian answered.

***

Within an hour Hugo and Pharrell were back at their hotel. Hugo was busy on the phone making arrangements with his bank for the money transfer. Meanwhile, Pharrell had fallen asleep after too much Vodka. When Pharrell eventually awoke, he was surprised to see Hugo in conversation again, on the phone, and hear the words, "see you in Paris" before ending the phone call.

"You have been asleep for over an hour. I have just made arrangements to see an American dealer in Paris in three days' time," Hugo remarked and then continued. "I hope that is okay with you, *mon cher ami*?"

"Yes and no, I was planning to see Angelique in Thailand when we wrap up the business here," replied Pharrell, as he tried to fully adjust his eyes to the fading light of the room. He could see across the balcony the distant vista in shadow as the sun had begun to set.

"How long do you plan to be in Paris…Hugo?" Pharrell asked abruptly annoyed with Hugo's current plans to fly to Paris and not to return to Bangkok as previously planned.

"A few days…perhaps, a week at most, it all depends on how negotiations go with the American. I need you there for back up. And, besides, you can always phone Angelique and explain the situation before we leave Algeria," he said cheekily, his blue eyes were bright like a twinkling star with a broad smile curling between his moustache and his beard hoping Pharrell would eventually agree to his new plans.

After a prolonged discussion, Pharrell reluctantly agreed to accompany Hugo to Paris. Later that evening, Pharrell phoned Angelique and was surprised to find out that she had booked out of the hotel and had left a brief message with the hotel reception for him. She explained in the message her editor wanted her back in America to cover another story, and she would phone him from America. Pharrell felt disappointed, he wanted to say so much to her, he had missed the chance to say how he loved her and he hoped she felt the same.

***

The next day, Hugo had received confirmation from his bank that the money transfer had gone through as expected. Hugo and Pharrell were in a taxi on their way to meet Oleg at his shop and pick up the papyri that afternoon. When they arrived at the shop Oleg was there to greet them. Oleg offered them some refreshments, but Hugo declined saying he had booked an evening flight and was eager to pick up the papyri and get back to the hotel as soon as possible. After Hugo had inspected the papyri and was satisfied that the papyri was the same as the one they had seen the other day Hugo and Pharrell shook hands with the Russian and then made their way back to their hotel in the taxi. Pharrell noticed the Russian's face had a reddish glow, probably celebrating with vodka the deal again and one hundred and twenty five thousand dollars in his back pocket, not bad for day's work, he whispered to himself.

"Hopefully, the American will buy it," Hugo said to Pharrell as they both carefully examined the document again in their room at the hotel.

"It's a big risk, for big rewards."

"That's a lot of money a quarter of a million dollars for a few pages of papyrus, Hugo."
"I don't intend to let this out of my sight, until, we meet with the American in Paris. It's going in my hand luggage…I don't trust the airline not to lose my luggage…its happened to me before," Hugo explained.
"I would be the same…Hugo. It's worth too much money to take a chance."
"What about the border customs?" Pharrell enquired, he wasn't sure if Hugo wanted to be reminded or not about what he was about to do. Hugo was taking a risk…a risk he wasn't prepared to do; regardless of the predictable time delay.
"It would take too long to get an export license. Besides, I have never been stopped before," Hugo countered, eyeing his friend like a lion stalking their prey ready to leap into action. "Don't worry it's my risk and my money, I will take all the responsibility."

***

At the airport departure lounge Hugo and Pharrell waited patiently for their flight boarding to be announced. In the meantime, Pharrell rang Angelique in America and was told by a colleague that she was out of the office, so Pharrell asked, if he could leave a message for Angelique. He decided he would keep the message short and simple, it just said; *I will be in Paris for few days…phone me…love Pharrell.*
"You must be in love, *mon cher ami*," Hugo said rhetorically having overheard his friend's message to Angelique on the phone.
Hugo's remark brought a beaming smile from Pharrell. "Yes, I think I am…it's been a long time since I felt this way. I just hope Angelique feels the same. Otherwise, it's going to be a brief relationship or

friendship." Pharrell knew as soon as he had said the word friendship that friendships between opposite sexes never usually work out. Was Hugo trying to deceive him or Angelique, he wondered.
"When will you see her again?"
"It all depends…what do you know about the American dealer?" Pharrell asked abruptly eager to change the conversation; he didn't feel comfortable talking about his love life, especially, when he wasn't sure himself if it was just a friendship or more.
"Not much…he has an office in New York and he represents some of the largest and wealthiest museums in America, such as the Guggenheim. His name is Harry Lebervitz. I was introduced to him through a friend some years ago when I was selling a sixteenth century book by Giorgio Vasari the Italian biographer of Leonardo di Vinci. He is no fool as you would expect…and he always tries to get a bargain. But, aren't we all like that as dealers."
Pharrell nodded his head with agreement, and then inquired. "Have you discussed a price on the papyri with him?"
"No, not yet, there's plenty of time, be patient, *mon cher ami*."

***

As Hugo and Pharrell made their way from Charles de Gaul airport to the Hotel Francis through the busy streets of Paris the taxi driver avoided the main avenues of traffic preferring the quieter back streets. Hugo told Pharrell that he had stayed at the hotel many times before, and that the hotel had an excellent reputation for quality food and comfort. He said the hotel was situated in the old quarter of Paris near the *boulevard du artiste* an area of small cafés and restaurants. It was the place, he said where many of the impressionist painters of the nineteenth century had lived and painted the local people who lived and frequented the area. He said that Henri de Toulouse-Lautrec's former studio was not far from the hotel and was now a museum and he promised Pharrell they would soon visit the artist's studio. Hugo told Pharrell that Ernest Hemingway also lived in the area when he was a young reporter for a newspaper and later wrote the 'Moveable Feast', which is a book about the author's early life in Paris in the 1920's.

"Have you read 'When the Bell Tolls,' it's about the Spanish Civil War?" Hugo asked.

"Yes…one of Hemingway's finest books…it's a classic," Pharrell replied.

"Are we near the hotel?"

"*Oui*, m*on cher ami*. Only, a few kilometres more, we are nearly there. Did you know that our hotel, the Hotel Francis is named after Saint Francis of Assisi who was the first person to record the same wounds as Jesus Christ the so called stigmata?"

"Yes, I have read about the saint before."

As the taxi approached the hotel Pharrell noticed the façade of the hotel. He saw the porch with gold letters displaying its name and the small sash windows above the entrance door. He saw the many cafés and restaurants on the boulevard that were busy as many people sat outside enjoying the afternoon sun.

Their room was on the second floor at the back of the hotel with a view of the hotel's garden and in the distance they could see the top of Eiffel Tower.

"At least I can get a good night's sleep here," Hugo remarked.

"Tomorrow, we meet with the America, so, tonight we can relax, and enjoy the fine cuisine the hotel has to offer, and then sample the night life on the *boulevard du artiste*."

"What about the papyri…will you take that with you tonight?" Pharrell asked.

"No, the hotel has a safe for valuables…I will store it there until tomorrow," Hugo responded with the confidence clearly audible in his voice.

Hugo told Pharrell that he had arranged for them to see Lucy Bouchard the professor of antiquities at the *University of Paris* for the following day. He wanted to show the papyri to Lucy before seeing the America to get her opinion on the original. Hugo explained that Lucy would take a small sample of the papyrus and send it to their lab for carbon dating.

"How long before we know the result of the carbon dating?" Pharrell queried at the same time thinking it could take several weeks.

"Lucy has promised no more than a week, she told me it would be a priority."

Hugo explained that he wanted to introduce an old friend, a man called Henri Piccar, who he said lived in a small village near where the famous battle of Agincourt took place. Hugo said his friend was an author and writer on early civilisations, who perhaps would know more about the ancient Babylonians' history.

Pharrell interrupted Hugo. "When will we visit with Henri Piccar?" He was now eager to know when they would go to see him. His quest was now lit again like a raging fire.

"*Oui, mon cher ami*, I have to make arrangements, but he's expecting us…I spoke with him before we departed from Algeria."

After storing the papyri in the hotel safe behind the main reception area Hugo and Pharrell wandered into the dining room and found a spare table and settled down to hear the hotel's hostess announce the celebration of a wedding anniversary. Bottles of wine had been provided on every table complements of the hotel.

"We wish Jean and Louise many more years of happiness together. Please raise your glasses in a toast to them. We also wish all our guests an enjoyable time at our hotel," the blond middle-age hostess announced.

In the dining room there were many families with children and many couples busy in their own world. Pharrell and Hugo could hear the voices of many different nationalities as they ordered their food from the pretty waitress. Hugo was keen for Pharrell to try some French cuisine, so he ordered for both of them.

"*Mon cher ami*, I think you will enjoy what I have ordered, it is a French delicacy. It is famous among the people of the north east region of France in the Rouine valley where some of the best wine is grown. They say that the nobles in the fifteenth century were the first to invent the recipe and then it became popular over the years throughout France for both rich and poor alike. Today, it's known as *ris de veau* and in English it's known as sweetbreads, but there is nothing sweet about them, and it's an acquired taste. Washed down with some excellent red wine from the Nancy region you will enjoy."

"You certainly enjoy your food and wine in France, it's a national pastime," Pharrell remarked. "You are certainly proof of that, Hugo."

"Oui, the French people like to savour their food and wine, much like the Spanish who take hours to have a meal. Not like the English and the Americans who eat and drink fast, and I guess that is why they like fast food outlets. To us, good food and wine is like making love, we like to take our time, and relish the occasion of eating among friends and family. The act of eating and drinking is a social event, a chance for young and old to come together and to pass time. You see, *mon cher ami*, the purpose of friendship and family is to experience what life has to offer together."

As Hugo continued talking, Pharrell's thoughts momentarily lingered on love. He wondered what Angelique was doing, was she enjoying the company of friends? He allowed his body to react to the thought of making love to her, he imagined for the first time what this perhaps would be like. He wanted to experience the same happiness he saw on the faces of the couple celebrating their wedding anniversary tonight in the hotel. He then began to have doubts. Did Angelique have the same passion for him? He was thinking too far ahead, he said to himself.

"It's like the Tour de France…,"

Pharrell interrupted, "What do you mean…it's like the Tour de France?"

Hugo realising Pharrell had not been listening and slightly annoyed with him explained why the Tour de France was so popular all over the world. Hugo explained its popularity was due to the bike race taking place over the course of three weeks and over many different types of terrain. The spectators watch a spectacle of endurance and become familiar with the many riders as the race progresses throughout different parts of France. The athletes in this bike race experience a supreme test of endurance, which captures the spectators' imagination of the courage needed combined with the racing skills to compete in such an event as the Tour de France.

"It's like the way we eat and drink, we like to take our time," Hugo said smiling. "That's why we take our time in preparing our food and even longer eating it adds to the pleasure not like the Americans and English."

After dinner they took a stroll down the boulevard outside the hotel and observed the night life amongst the many cafés and restaurants. They passed numerous restaurants and through their windows could see many people busily enjoying their evening cuisine. On the pavements outside cafés people sat and watched as the throng of tourists and Parisians ambled up and down the street. Hugo and Pharrell sat down outside a small café and ordered some coffee and from where they were seated could observe the crowds along the boulevard.

"What are you thinking about, *mon cher ami*?"

Pharrell thoughts at that moment were about Angelique, but he wanted to keep them private. He felt alone and empty as he saw families and couples pass by enjoying the evening. He sensed the jealousy inside himself when he saw couples holding hands as they walked by, he wanted the same. He wanted to be loved and to give love, and it was Angelique he wanted more than ever.

"Not much Hugo...What about you?" Pharrell replied, deciding to deflect the question and emphasise back to him. Pharrell decided to keep his thoughts to himself for time being. Hugo would probably realise he was thinking about Angelique, but that was alright, he thought.

"Tomorrow's business," Hugo answered with a profound voice like a captain of a sailing ship giving orders to his bosun to ahoy anchor. Hugo's brow was a cacophony of deep wrinkles matching the seriousness of his contemplation.

At that moment, Pharrell wondered if Hugo thought about Ning, but decided not to ask fearing the conversation perhaps would eventually turn towards how he felt about Angelique. A discussion about his relationship with Angelique was a subject he wanted to avoid for now, he mused.

"In the morning we will see Lucy and in the afternoon the American. It will be a busy day and hopefully a profitable one." Hugo remarked.

"What price are you going to ask the American to pay for the papyri?" Pharrell asked.

"Nothing...you are."

"What do you mean?"

"I want you to conduct the negotiations tomorrow with the American because he knows me and he doesn't know you. It will catch him off guard. I will act as your advisor and expert on the papyri. This way, we will hopefully achieve a higher price than we would if I was the seller. I know the American; he's a shrewd businessman and always wants a bargain and will try any trick to achieve it."

"Okay, so what price do I start the negotiations at?" Pharrell asked.

"What price do you think its worth?"

At that moment, the waiter arrived with their coffees and said, "*Ques sai volez vou?*" Hugo said no, and paid the waiter before waiting for Pharrell to reply.

"It all depends on the rarity and how much someone is willing to pay. But, from past experience I would say close to a million dollars if a collector or a museum wants it enough. But, at the moment we are not sure if it's genuine so the price is speculative and a major gamble that would affect its selling potential."

"I agree with your assessment Pharrell...we will know soon enough if it's genuine. Lucy has promised to get the radio carbon dating results to me within a week. We will also have her evaluation of the papyri tomorrow, which will help impress the American. I also think you should mention to the American that we have another potential buyer...the Louvre museum."

Pharrell looked puzzled and said, "Is that true, is the Louvre interested in the papyri?"

"No, not exactly true...*mon cher ami*. But, Lucy Bouchard is a member of a committee of antiquities at the Louvre. She has promised to contact other members on the committee, on the possibility of the Louvre buying the papyri should it turn out to be genuine. So, it would be worth mentioning to the American that we have the Louvre museum as another potential buyer. The American will like that; he is known to be greedy for success and he will want to secure the purchase of the papyri before someone else."

"Okay, I will mention the Louvre and see what happens tomorrow. What about the asking price...I mean, the minimum selling price you are willing to accept?" Pharrell asked intently waiting on every word.

"Let's see...," Hugo was busy thinking and purring like a cat, he thought about the risk he was taking and how much he could squeeze out of the American before answering Pharrell's question. "Let's say half million dollars...anything above that will be a bonus," Hugo responded with a wide grin on his face like he was admiring a beautiful woman.

Pharrell saw the satisfaction on Hugo's face and with a similar expression reiterated, "Okay, we are in agreement...we will see what transpires tomorrow."

They continued talking for some time while they sat there observing the people that passed by their table along the boulevard, until, the evening air had become cooler and they decided to head back for a late night drink in their hotel's bar.

On the walk back to the hotel Pharrell again turned his thoughts to Angelique. She had not phoned him since leaving Algeria. He wondered if she had received the message he had given to a colleague at her work place. Perhaps, she was too busy or not interested in him any longer, he thought.

At the hotel's bar Hugo and Pharrell were surprised to see how busy it was. There were a few couples in conversation on some tables and several patrons on bar stools, and one or two eyeing for the attention of the pretty blond hostess behind the bar.

The hostess said, "*Bonjour, ques que sai vouley vous?*"

Hugo waited for Pharrell to speak first, "Jac Daniels with Coke Cola and Ice, please."

Por oiu , "The same, Jac Daniels with Coke and ice, *Merci*."

The pretty hostess then said in English with an attractive smile aimed at Pharrell, "Have you had an enjoyable evening, Sir?"

Pharrell was not sure if the hostess was flirting or just making pleasant conversation. "Yes, thank you. I have enjoyed being a voyeur for the evening along the boulevard outside. It's a surprisingly busy street, with many couples and families with children wandering about." She looked surprised at Pharrell's comments, but then again, perhaps, not understanding what he meant.

The hostess said, "Oh, yes…that is because tonight is the eve of a national holiday tomorrow…Bastille Day."

"I see…I had forgotten completely what day of the month it was. Yes, I know how important Bastille Day is to France. I should have realised why the boulevard was so busy tonight." And with a smile directed at the hostess, Pharrell returned the compliment and they took their drinks and sat down at a nearby table. Pharrell was deep in his thoughts.

"It's strange."

"What's strange?" Hugo asked abruptly eager to know what Pharrell was thinking about.

"How you suddenly become attractive to the opposite sex…when you start to have feelings for someone. It's like you have an invisible halo or something similar that sends a signal to women that you are available and worth capturing. Whereas before, when I was single and had no interest in a woman…nothing came my way. It seems you unexpectedly become hot property." His emotions were lucid, and caused by the effects of the wine he had consumed earlier that day, he mused.

"Yes, I understand what you mean. It's a universal law of nature. They call it the 'law of attraction' or something similar. When you think about something enough then you start to send signals across the universe. It's then that you are given choices, so your destiny can be written. Some people say that the universe of nature is then testing you, by giving you a choice to see what it is you really want. This is how the law of attraction works."

"You seem to know a lot about this law of attraction, where did you read this?" Pharrell asked.

"I didn't, Ning told me about it soon after we met. She said one day while at work in the tourist information office in Bangkok, she had found a book that must have been mislaid by a tourist that day. Later that day, when no one had come back to the office to claim their book, she decided she would take it home and read it before bringing it back the next day in case someone claimed the book. She said she was fascinated by what the book had to say because it was similar to how Buddhists believe in their faith how you should conduct yourself.

She went on to say that in her prays she hoped to meet a man that would love and take care of her and that is all she wanted."
"What was the book called?"
"The book is called, 'The Secret'," Hugo replied.
"Did you read the book?"
"No, I didn't need to, Ning told me enough about it and besides I have always believed that with the right attitude you can accomplish anything. Jesus said that you reap what you sow."
"I didn't realise you were religious, Hugo?"
"As a boy, I attended a Catholic school. My mother and father were devoted Catholics and wanted me to be a priest. But, I didn't want to. So, when I finished school I went straight to university and studied literature. I don't think my parents ever forgave me, but they understood my reasons…or should I say they had to accept my decision. You see, I learned a lot about religion at school and decided I didn't like the doctrine that went with following a faith. I believe in God, but not in a religion. Jesus never mentioned religion when he talked to those who would listen, so why should I follow a religion…it's all just doctrine made up to control the people."
Pharrell gently nodded his head with agreement. And decided he would change the subject of the conversation. The conversation was getting too deep and personal, he thought.

***

It was July fourteenth Bastille Day, a national public holiday to celebrate the fall of the monarchy in 1789 and the dawn of the French republic as Hugo and Pharrell sat in their taxi observing the passing crowds as they travelled across the suburbs of Paris towards the home of the Professor Lucy Bouchard.

Hugo and Pharrell saw how the taxi driver had to avoid the main roads at the centre of Paris and who occasionally cursed in French at the detours he had to make. The Champs- ELysees would be completely blocked from regular traffic that day to allow for the procession of service men and women who would be parading along the road in celebration of Bastille Day later that afternoon.

The home of the professor was situated in the north-eastern district of a Paris suburb called *St. Marks du Lille* named after the patron saint and the national emblem of France the *fleur du Lille*. Hugo knew the area and announced, "We are in the St Marks district...Lucy's home town." Pharrell noticed it was a leafy and prosperous area with many substantial houses set in their own manicured and well-kept gardens with plenty of space between them.

As the taxi drove down the many tree lined avenues the taxi eventually slowed and turned into a driveway leading to a gothic style house with several turrets to its façade. And in the front garden was a water fountain in full flow feeding a pond of water lilies. Finally, the taxi's satellite navigation system announced in French that they had arrived at their destination.

Lucy was already waiting at the front of her home leaning on a gothic arched door ready to greet them before Hugo and Pharrell got out of the taxi. Pharrell noticed how attractive the middle-age brunette was dressed. He saw her generous smile beneath the dark rimmed glasses she wore that did not detract from the beauty of her middle-eastern complexion, he thought.

"*Bonjour*," she said, greeting Hugo with a kiss to his cheeks and a hug.

"This is my friend Pharrell," he said to her, while she greeted Pharrell with the same embrace and kiss that she had given to Hugo.

"Please come in."

They followed Lucy through the hallway where they passed a beautiful ornate and carved wooden staircase into a room filled with antique furniture and books that lined the walls. Pharrell enjoyed the smell of old books and the antique furniture he immediately felt at home and yet, he missed the same comfort of his shop in Stavanger, Norway.

"Please, make yourselves comfortable. I will fetch some refreshments for us from the kitchen."

Hugo and Pharrell sat down in front of a huge bay window that showered the room with the morning light. As they waited for Lucy to return, they relaxed, and started to think. Pharrell wondered if Lucy was married, she was too attractive not be married, he thought. And Hugo was thinking about the first time he met Lucy at university when he was a teenager, he perhaps should have proposed marriage when he had the chance, he thought.

As they all sat there and drank their coffee Hugo placed the leather binder that held the papyri in front of Lucy for her perusal.

From where Pharrell was sat, he could observe Lucy's every move. He noticed her olive skin and wondered if she had Spanish or Italian blood. He saw her dark brown eyes glisten and a smile appear around her lips as she turned the pages of the binder. He wondered what she was thinking. Did she think the papyri were genuine, now, that she had the original in her hands, he thought.

As Lucy read the Greek and Aramaic words and lettering, she took off her glasses and gently flicked her hair like a model before being photographed and asked, "Does this correspond to the copy you sent to me, Hugo?"

"Yes exactly. I have also brought a copy of the original translation you sent me. Do you want to see it?"

Lucy responded, "Yes, okay…let me see the translation." As she examined the translation and cross checked each piece of papyrus, she was confident that she had made no mistakes in the translation, she surmised.

After several minutes of silence Hugo was impatient to know what Lucy's was thinking. "Well…what do you think Lucy?" Hugo asked exasperated.

Lucy's eyes momentarily looked up above her dark rimmed spectacles and stared at Hugo briefly before continuing her examination of the papyri. Hugo's impatience was an evident characteristic even in his maturity, age had not mellowed him, and she mused.

Pharrell had not noticed Hugo's frustration before, perhaps, he guessed the huge sum of money Hugo had gambled on the purchase of the papyri was beginning to unsettle him, it would test most people's patience to the limit, and he mused, even himself.

After several more minutes, and, for Hugo and Pharrell what appeared ages during the silence waiting for Lucy to finish her examination of the papyri, she announced that she was satisfied she had not made any mistakes in her original translation of the papyri.

"Everything appears okay, so far," she remarked.

Hugo asked bewildered at what Lucy had said, "What do you mean…so far?"

Lucy replied, "As I mentioned before, when you sent me a copy of the papyri, I said that the formation and use of language structure is consistent with that era. But that doesn't prove the papyri are not a forgery. Yes, it's difficult to fake, but these days almost anything can be faked to such a level of expertise that even an expert can be fooled."

"Yes, of course…we already know all of that," Hugo responded annoyed that Lucy perhaps was playing games with him because of their past history together. She had chosen the right time to show her annoyance with him in front of Pharrell, he thought.

"Be patient Hugo…I have not finished my analysis," she said, raising her voice at him like a school teacher reprimanding a pupil for being naughty.

"Okay, go on," he said frustrated at Lucy's demeanour, as sweat started to appear across his forehead and trickle down the side of his face. Hugo was like a man on death row waiting for the inevitable.

"I will need to take samples of the papyri that will mean a sample from each papyrus and also a sample of the ink on each papyrus to be absolutely sure. When we have the radio carbon dating results and the analysis of the formulation of ink used, we can then make a final assessment of the likelihood of its authenticity."

"Okay, let's do it," Hugo said, eagerly wanting the process to end as soon as possible. Lucy and Pharrell noticed the frustration in Hugo's demeanour and could not avoid seeing how much sweat had soiled his shirt from the heat of the sun's rays, which was more intense as the morning progressed, and his obvious anxiety concerning his purchase of the papyri was clearly visible across his forehead of wrinkles and sweat. It was a lot of money to lose if it turned out to be a fake and perhaps, even worse, he would look like a fool to his long-time friend Lucy.

Hugo and Pharrell followed Lucy into an adjacent room where she placed the binder containing the papyri on an old oak kneehole table. They watched as Lucy sat down and carefully started to tease the first piece of papyrus from its protective see-through plastic cover. They saw how Lucy cut away a small sample of papyrus with a utility knife and then carefully scratched at a section of the ink lettering and then collected the dust into an envelope. Lucy then labelled the samples and continued the process of cutting away a section of papyrus and scraping a section of ink lettering from each piece of the papyri.

"That's it...I have labelled each sample A and B and I have taken samples from each of the four papyrus sections. Tomorrow, I will send these samples by courier to the carbon dating laboratory in Grenoble," Lucy stated, as she looked above her glasses at Hugo and Pharrell staring down at her.

"When will you have the results?" Hugo asked with the impatience of a dog in heat. He had invested a fortune and risked his reputation, he needed results fast. He hoped Lucy had forgotten the past at least for now.

"Hopefully, within a few days...I will stress that it's urgent. That's the best I can do...the rest is up to the technicians at the lab," she replied.

Hugo glanced at his wristwatch and said, "We have to be going soon, we have an appointment with a potential buyer."

"So soon...I have made a light lunch for you and Pharrell. And besides, we need to discuss my fee." At that moment, Lucy had a glee in her manner, such a way as a red robin sings in the morning, tuneful, and pronouncing another glorious day of sunshine.

"Okay, that's fine."

As Hugo and Pharrell sat down in the lounge waiting for Lucy to return with the food, they heard the sound of a man's voice call out to Lucy. Pharrell immediately assumed it was Lucy's husband and Hugo was thinking the same.

Moments later, Lucy returned from the kitchen holding a tray with some wine and sandwiches and placed it upon a coffee table in front of them. She then announced with joy in her manner, that her son had just returned from his girlfriend's apartment and would be in shortly to introduce himself.

Hugo realised, now, was not the time to ask questions, he was not about to pry into Lucy's past, he said to himself. But, he was curious nonetheless, he wondered if Lucy had finally tied the knot. She was a beautiful woman, with the mystery of her Mediterranean features adding a lure most men would find attractive and get hopelessly hooked.

"Finally," she said, as she introduced her son to Hugo and Pharrell. "This is Thierry my son." They could see the likeness in him to his mother as they took turns to shake hands with him. "He's a student at the University of Paris studying to be an architect," she proudly announced, while her son blushed with embarrassment and then made his apologies before leaving the room.

As all three sat round the coffee table and ate their food and drank their wine Pharrell decided he would change the topic of conversation. "Lucy, have you heard about the '*Shahbla el Allah*' believed to have been written by the ancient Babylonians?"

"Yes, I have…and to be precise. It was written first by the Sumerians, and then most scholars believe updated by the Babylonians and it has been lost to history for about two and half thousand years," she replied.

"Why do you want to know?"

"It's been a quest for me…to find the '*Shahbla el Allah*' since I first heard about it, many moons ago. I just wondered what you perhaps knew."

"So, you are a treasure seeker…an eternal optimist," she remarked, as Pharrell smiled and nodded his head in agreement.

"All I know…you probably already know. The *'Shahbla el Allah'* is mentioned on many Babylonian and Sumerian cuneiform clay tablets that have been found so far, and also in some ancient Greek papyrus texts. That is why scholars are confident the *'Shahbla el Allah'* did exist. It's probably buried somewhere…and possibly one day it will be found like the Dead Sea Scrolls. You could research the Greek writer Herodotus who travelled to Babylon about one hundred years after King Nebuchadnezzar died and wrote an account of what he saw in Babylon. Perhaps, you will find some clues about the *'Shahbla el Allah'* from what Herodotus wrote about Babylon at around that time. It's more than likely, a Greek copy of the text is buried in a grave somewhere, just waiting…for a treasure hunter to discover it."

"Thanks for your optimism…I always fancied myself as I grave digger," Pharrell said laughing.

Hugo interrupted the conversation and said, "Lucy, you said that you have a contact at the Louvre. What's his or her name and contact details?"

"His name is Michel Napier and I will give you his phone number before you leave," she replied.

***

"Here are the names of the two I want you to follow… including the hotel they are staying at. I want you to follow them discretely, and give me a report daily of who they see and where they go. No matter what time of day or night, I need to be kept informed…is that understood?" It was like David and Goliath as they looked at each other for the first time, not knowing if there was any trust between each other. Harry Lebervitv, a jewish art dealer was small in stature, who had made his way up in life from the hard knock streets of Brooklyn , New York, to the money streets of Manhattan famed for being the business and financial centre of America if not the world.

As the former French legionnaire, a giant of a man, now, as a private detective, he read the piece of paper his new employer Harry Lebervitz had given him, he soon realised, from the luxury surroundings of the Hilton hotel that he could ask for more money. Paris is an expensive city, but the Hilton meant money, lots of money. This new assignment felt like a lot of money was involved somehow, and not the typical jobs he had done since leaving the French foreign legion. He now made a living following errant husbands and wives committing adultery, but, he could almost smell the money, the detective said to himself.

"I need to know why…why you want me to follow them. It's purely for legal issues as a private detective you understand this?" the detective inquired.

Harry looked at the man in front of him, and guessed from his physique that here was a man who had served his country. Most likely, he presumed, in the celebrated Foreign Legion from his stature and his dark complexion and brown almost black eyes typically Corsican features. Harry decided to tell him only what he needed to know. The prospect of divulging too much unsettled him. From previous experience when it came to money…a lot of money, people change and not always for the good, he surmised.

"Yes, you do need to know…and know this; I am not the type of person you cross." He had a scowl written on the lines of his face, every wrinkle protruding. "I'm making a bid for a rare document. So, I need to know if I have competitors or not. Is that sufficient for French legal issues, as you say? Now, is everything *kosher*?" Harry calmly asked hoping the detective had finished his interrogation.

The detective nodded his head and said, "Yes, that is fine Mr. Lebervitz. Now, about payment and expenses on this assignment, I charge two hundred euros per day plus expenses is that…"

Harry interrupted the detective and handed him an envelope. "Here is two thousand euros to get you started. Now, if I'm happy with your work and progress then there will be a bonus on completion. Now, do we have a deal?"

Harry saw the look of gratification on the detective's face as they shook hands. When it came to money and the prospect of more money Harry knew how to make a deal, it came natural to him. The days growing up in the Bronx, New York had taught him that survival instinct. He had the detective in his pocket for now, he mused.

"When do I start?" the detective asked.

"Now…tonight, I want to know what these guys get up to day and night. Here is my phone number and you can always leave a message for me at reception. Now, if I need to contact you away from your office what are your details?"

The detective handed Harry a business card. "Call me anytime on that number Mr. Lebervitz day or night. And, you can call me Jac if you wish." Jac was hoping for an amiable reaction from Harry, but Harry Lebervitz had other ideas, he was not the man to mix business with friendship.

"Ok, just remember, I need to know daily what these guys are up to, without fail. So, start tonight at their hotel."
The detective nodded his head and smiled at Harry as he turned to leave Harry's hotel room. Jac had a feeling this new assignment was going to be a profitable job, people that stay at the Hilton always had more money to spend, otherwise, they would stay in cheaper hotels, he was thinking.

***

"Change of plan…we are meeting the American at the Hilton hotel," said Hugo. Hugo explained to Pharrell as they sat in the taxi on their way to the hotel that he had changed the meeting place from the Louvre to the Hilton because of the public holiday.
"Are we meeting him in his hotel room?"
"No, in the bar at the hotel…it's safer and more people about."
"Don't forget what we discussed the other night about the asking price and your role as the negotiator." Hugo repeated to Pharrell his instructions while Pharrell occasionally nodded his head in agreement, but his mind was elsewhere. Angelique had not phoned him; perhaps, she never received the message from her colleague at work, he mused.
Along the boulevard as the taxi pulled up outside the Hilton hotel Hugo and Pharrell noticed a crowd had gathered in the distance at the intersection with the Champs Elysees. "It's because Bastille Day their waiting there to watch the parade go by," Hugo remarked.

As they walked into the hotel's bar Hugo looked around before noticing the American dealer sat alone, at a table, near a window facing the boulevard. Hugo was disappointed. He had expected to see Harry's partner. Perhaps, she is busy watching the parade with the rest of the crowd at the end of the street, he thought.
"This is Harry Lebervitz…Harry this is Pharrell Anderson my associate," Hugo said, while Pharrell and Harry shook hands. Hugo and Pharrell then sat down opposite Harry and Hugo quickly called the waitress over to their table and ordered a round of drinks.
"Where is your partner…today Harry," Hugo asked candidly.
"She decided to walk to the end of the road and watch the parade go by. She likes all that pomp and ceremony on a day like today…Bastille Day. The day the French people revolted against the aristocracy and became a republic. Hopefully, I will see her return before we finish our negotiations here because I value her opinion," Harry replied.
Hugo handed over the leather binder enclosing the papyri to Harry. "Here…you have the papyri and an English translation of the Greek and Aramaic text for each of the papyrus," Hugo said to Harry while gesturing to Pharrell to take over proceedings.
Pharrell waited several minutes observing every move, and carefully paid more attention to every facial expression on Harry's face like sizing up your opponents at a poker table before beginning his negotiations with him. "What do you think?" Pharrell asked inquisitively.
"Do you have any evidence that it's genuine?" Harry immediately responded with a question, while he stroked his beard and waited for an answer.

"Yes, we have the expert opinion of a professor at the University of Paris plus our own expertise in this field," Pharrell remarked.

"And what field is that?"

Pharrell quickly replied, "I have over twenty years' experience as a dealer in ancient manuscripts and antiquarian books."

"Okay, continue," Harry grunted.

"We have also taken samples of the papyrus for carbon dating and should have the results within a few days."

"What is your asking price?" Harry asked candidly.

"One million dollars would seem to be the going rate. I should also tell you that we have another potential buyer," Pharrell remarked with the authority of a school teacher with confidence and knowledge with no sign of nerves.

There were several minutes of silence before it was broken by the sound of ice rattling in glasses as the waitress arrived with their drinks. "Would you like anything else," she said in broken English, before scurrying away to serve another table.

Pharrell observed the waitress on another table and could hear her speaking in French. She must have heard us talking in English earlier and decided to speak in English not her native French for our convenience. A pleasant gesture on her part, he pondered.

Pharrell waited for Harry to speak first. Pharrell learned early on selling books to collectors that it was best to let the collectors do all the talking and wait for their reaction to the price. His experience from an early age in Norway selling books from his parent's antique shop taught him to always keep his mouth shut and wait for the customer to talk first. Usually, it resulted in a successful sale, he mused.

"Your other potential buyer…who is it?" Harry asked hardheartedly not expecting a positive answer.

Pharrell waited several seconds before giving an answer. "I cannot tell you his or her name at the moment, because it wouldn't be fair or indeed good business practice. But I'm willing to say the Louvre museum has expressed an interest in purchasing the papyri."

"Okay…I see. You want to auction the papyrus…is that it?" Harry replied annoyed and disappointed. He was annoyed, that the Louvre could take his prize with a higher bid. He felt the stress and hoped Hugo and Pharrell could see the look of disappointment on his face amongst the deep worry wrinkles from a lifetime of expensive acquisitions.

"No, that is not what I said. You have first option on the purchase. If you decline then Hugo and I will offer the papyri to the Louvre museum," Pharrell said calmly.

"Okay, when will you have the results of the carbon dating?" Harry asked gesturing to Hugo and Pharrell with open hands for answers.

"Hopefully, within a few days, no more than a week at most we should have the results of the carbon dating."

"You can also have the phone details of Lucy Bouchard the professor at the University to Paris…if you wish?" Hugo interrupted.

Pharrell slightly annoyed at the interruption said, "Yes, Lucy Bouchard is an expert on ancient papyrus and Greek and Aramaic text. She gave Hugo and me an excellent analysis of the papyri and it was worth every penny." Pharrell decided to inform Harry that Lucy's expertise cost money in a roundabout way without revealing how much. Harry would either use someone else as the expert or rely on Lucy's knowledge depending on how much he valued her views, he surmised.

"Let's talk price…if everything is *Kosher* with the papyri I would like to make an offer. But, first I need some time to think and besides I would like my partner to view the papyri. And, for some reason she is not back yet, so perhaps we can arrange to see you when you have the results of the carbon dating in a few days' time," Harry said smiling.

"Yes, that is fine…but what is your offer?" Pharrell asked again.

"I would like a discount of say ten to twenty percent of the asking price. I have to make a profit…you can understand this…Yes. We all have to make a profit that is how the world turns…my son. *Kosher*…you understand this. Yes..?" Harry asked politely in his Jewish manner.

"I never understand women, one minute to the next they nag you…and then they disappear for hours. I wanted my partner to take a look at this," Harry continued explaining his thoughts.

"But, you are interested in a discount that is okay. We will discuss terms then," Pharrell replied.

Hugo suddenly interrupted the conversation by reminding Pharrell that they had another appointment that afternoon. They were both soon in a taxi on their way to Agincourt.

***

"Harry looked disappointed when you interrupted the negotiations. Was it a ploy, Hugo?" Pharrell asked curiously.

"Yes and no. *Mon cher ami*…It's a long drive to Agincourt…about 400 kilometres from Paris. Luckily, we started in the outskirts of Paris…but it will take the

taxi driver about three hours or so, and without stops to get there. I prefer to get to Henri's place in daylight…and I'm sure he does as well," Hugo replied.
"Do you mean the taxi driver?"
"No…*mon cher ami*. I mean Henri… he told me last night on the phone, since the robbery …he was nervous at night."
"What robbery?"
"He was robbed at knife point…late one night last winter. Henri didn't go into details about the robbery…Just instructions on how to get to his place," Hugo explained.
Pharrell decided to keep the conversation going, and besides the journey to Agincourt would seem quicker if they talked, he thought. "Tell me, how long have you known Henri?"
"I can't blame him for being nervous…after being robbed at knife point. Knowing Henri like I do. Henri is an old friend from my youth. We met at university. We became friends then and have kept in touch over the years. He can be eccentric sometimes though. I remember one day, he arrived at our university dressed as a woman. I believe many fellow students were both shocked and laughing at this event at the time," Hugo continued explaining Henri's characteristics while actively observing the passing traffic. The main roads were packed with tourists for Bastille Day, a happy holiday for many travellers, he thought. His thoughts continued to linger on his youth growing up in a small village as he explained the reasons why he preferred the countryside.
"Oh, *mon cher*, by the way…it was a ploy. I interrupted you because I wanted the America to think we had another serious buyer. Harry Lebervitz is the kind of dealer who is greedy and shrewd at the same time. It's

good for Harry to believe he has competition," Hugo explained.
"You could have told me before...I felt exposed," Pharrell said annoyingly.
"Sorry, Pharrell...sometimes it's better you don't know...it's more realistic. *Mon cher.*"
"Next time tell me...otherwise, there won't be another time," Pharrell said in anger. Pharrell had decided he had enough of Hugo's antics. Increasingly, he had doubts about his relationship with Hugo. There were times when he hated being with him, he thought.
"I can't wait to see Angelique..."
"That's why you probably hate me right know...You long to see her. Is that right?" Hugo asked.
As Pharrell thought, for a moment, he noticed through the taxi window some holidaymakers parked by the side of the road in a picnic area. Perhaps one day that could be Angelique and him enjoying the countryside together, he mused.
"How long before we arrive at Agincourt?" Deciding not to reply to the previous question, Pharrell was keen to change the subject of the conversation.
"We should arrive in an hour or so...we are in a region of France known for its fine beer. Did you known that the famous and world renowned *bières du nord* is produced not far from here. The French Kings and Queens were the first to grow hops and barley for beer. The safest thing to drink back then...you couldn't trust the water, so people drank beer and wine," Hugo replied.
"Hugo...what was that river we just crossed over?"
"*Mon cher*...that is the Somme river, that gives life to this region of France."

"This talk about rivers, wine and water is given me a thirst, that I need to quench," Hugo said licking his lips. "A glass of beer or wine would do right now."
"Do you think the '*Shahbla el Allah*' exists?" Pharrell asked.
"Why, are you having doubts?"
"No, I'm just interested in what your opinion is."
"Remember, if you believe it exists then that's all that matters. *Mon cher*."
"Hugo…Tell me what you think?" Pharrell frustratingly asked again.
"Remember, every legend has some truth…and the truth never lies. A legend passes down the centuries from mouth to mouth, until, eventually; someone records the words in a written language. Each time the legend gets translated from one language to another the scribe can misinterpret the meaning of certain words, and so a new legend is born. Recently, the story in the Bible of Moses parting the Red Sea was found to be a misinterpretation of the word…*reeds*. It was the reeds that Moses parted not the Red Sea. A far more plausible story, but not a miracle we were all led to believe for so long. So, you see *mon cher*, the fact that other documents exist that mention *Shahbla el Allah*, we can assume that a legend exists and from that the quest to find the proof is the *raison d'etre*."
"Do you agree with what Lucy Bouchard said about *Shahbla el Allah*?" Pharrell asked, while trying to avoid thoughts about the discomfort of the taxi journey. Momentarily, his thoughts were of Angelique. Why had Angelique not phoned him since Algeria?
"Lucy didn't really say much…only that she had heard the legend about *Shahbla el Allah*. And that other papyri and ancient written text mention its existence. And perhaps one day a copy of *Shahbla el Allah* will

turn up in an excavated grave of a deceased priest. That's when she said to you, about you, being a grave digger," Hugo replied laughing.

"Yes, I found that amusing as well…she certainly has a sense of humour that woman," Pharrell said grinning at Hugo's laughter. And also a nice pair of legs to match her vivacity, he thought.

Pharrell decided not to ask Hugo any questions on his past relationship with Lucy. Besides, Hugo would say if he wanted to, he thought. "How far before we get to Henri's home…Hugo?"

"Have patience, *mon cher*, we are almost there."

The sound of gravel churning as the taxi car pulled into the driveway of Henri's home were over shadowed by the barks and growls of Henri's dogs as Hugo and Pharrell glimpsed the seclusion of the surroundings, and all they could see for miles around were green fields. Pharrell remarked to Hugo that it was like a scene from a story by the Brothers Grimm. Henri's home was secluded there was no doubt; it was no wonder it had been a target for burglars. The brandy and dark rum colour Rottweilers that greeted the taxi as it pulled up in front of the imposing cottage looked friendly enough with Henri around, but on their own they would terrify most people.

Henri Piccar was at the front door of the thatched cottage, he had heard the commotion of the dogs barking and the sound of gravel churning as the taxi pulled into his driveway. Henri was immaculately groomed that suited his years with his grey hair thinning, but well cut and greased that suited his Mediterranean tan and his blue eyes of someone who had had an easier life than most.

"*Salut*! This is my good friend Pharrell. Henri this is Pharrell Anderson the person I told you about on the phone. As they shook hands Pharrell immediately felt at ease, he could see a friendly face ready to welcome him into his home. Hugo greeted Henri with the *faire la bise* reserved for close friends. Hugo and Pharrell noticed the thatch cottage had a pleasant smell of the countryside, an aroma of cut flowers lingered in the air. Henri's cottage had been richly decorated with modern art and antique furniture that suited the low ceilings and the faintly lit interior provided by the small sash windows. Pharrell immediately, felt cool, he had stopped sweating after being caged like a pet bird in the back of the taxi with Hugo for several hours. Pharrell noticed the thick walls of the cottage provided a cool haven away from the heat and humidity of the late afternoon. The author's home did indeed provide an agreeable and creative space to write books, Pharrell mused.

"This is my wife, Cherie." She was just as well-groomed as her husband with her bleach blond hair styled into a bun with the same Mediterranean tan and deep blue eyes with an attractive high cheekbone face.

"We have prepared some food and wine for you," Henri said.

Hugo and Pharrell sat down separately in the floral decorated armchairs, leaving the couch for the couple. In front of them was a large open fireplace ready with wood and kinder to be lit on a cold evening. They both waited patiently for the couple to return.

Hugo said, "What do you think, *mon cher?*"

Pharrell replied, "At the moment, just glad to be sat in a comfy armchair and not cooped up on the back seat of that taxi. I'm sure I felt every bump in the road on my *derriere*."

Hugo laughing said, "Yes, the journey took its toll on me, too. I think we should take the train back...it would be more comfortable on both our *derriere's*."

"That's the best suggestion you have made all day...Hugo."

Their laughter caught the ear of Henri as he and his wife returned with the food and wine. "What are you both laughing about, please tell?" Henri asked curiously.

"We have decided to take the train back to Paris rather than the arduous discomfort on our *derrieres* in the back of a taxi," Hugo explained, as they all laughed. "Besides, the train journey from here takes about one hour to Paris compared to over three hours in a taxi. I don't know why I didn't think to take the train? Anyway, we are here that's the main thing...we arrived safely."

"Do you have the papyri with you, Hugo?"

Hugo replied enthusiastically eager to hear what his friend's views were, "Yes, here you are...take a look and tell me what you both think?"

Henri and Cherie carefully opened the leather binder containing the papyri. They took several minutes reading the translation and analysing each papyrus before muttering a single word. Hugo and Pharrell noticed the delight on their faces as each papyrus was carefully examined. Most people find a piece of history exciting and I just hope it's genuine, Hugo thought. Pharrell was preoccupied observing their reactions; he saw Henri's and Cherie's facial expressions of excitement as they turned each page of the papyri, and he wondered if they thought the same as him. Did Henri and Cherie have the same doubts about its authenticity as he had? Perhaps, the disappointment of not hearing from Angelique this past week was clouding his judgement, Pharrell supposed.

"It's an interesting piece of history," Henri broke the silence.

"Yes, I agree, but is it genuine?" Cherie asked.

Hugo replied briskly annoyed at the suggestion, "We will know in a few days. We have sent samples for carbon dating. Until then we have just speculation and conjecture as to its authenticity.

Henri said, "Sorry, if my wife was blunt, but it's a question most people would ask at some point because there are so many fakes on the market.

Cherie interrupted, "Just about everything you can think of these days is being faked...from perfume to artwork. The criminals have their hands in many different pies. But forgery goes back to the medieval times when religious relics were faked to provide income for their churches and monasteries. Take for example the Shroud of Turin that has been scrutinised and examined by scientists and been found to date from medieval times and not from the time of the death of Jesus Christ."

Hugo said, "You are right, of course...but so far all the omens are good. We have the analysis of a professor of antiquities at the University of Paris. Also, the many years of experience Pharrell and myself have gained in the trade of antiquarian books and documents to guide us."

Henri asked, "What does the professor say about the papyri?"

Hugo replied, "The professor made a detailed examination of the structure of the language used and found that the Greek and Aramaic script would be difficult to fake and indeed is contemporary with the time...about two and a half thousand years ago. You have read the professor's translation...word for word. The papyri document is assumed to be written by a priest who is recording a legend about the Phoenician traders who sailed the Mediterranean trading with many different people. We believe the legend was originally handed down by word of mouth from generation to generation until it was written down...we assume by a priest or scribe of some sort. The legend we believe derives from the ancient Sumerians and handed down to the Babylonians who traded with the Phoenicians at that time. That is the essence of what the professor concluded."

Henri replied, "An interesting conclusion and legends are very intriguing from a writer's point of view."

Cherie said laughing, "Don't get him started...he'll want to start another book on the subject before you leave."

As they chatted, Pharrell decided to interrupt the conversation. He wanted to know what Henri knew about his quest. He wondered what Hugo had told Henri. What did Henri know about *Shahbla el Allah*, he said to himself? "Sorry, to interrupt, but what do you know about my quest to find the missing book of God...believed to have originated in Babylon in ancient times?"

Before Henri or Cherie could reply, Hugo interrupted and said, "Henri and Cherie have already prepared a document for you...with all the knowledge they have and where you perhaps will find more. I didn't tell you before Pharrell, because I wanted to surprise you."

Pharrell said, "It's a nice surprise, Hugo. It feels like my birthday, but it's not. I would rather hear what Henri and Cherie may know about my quest verbally; otherwise, I perhaps would overlook an important aspect in just reading facts in a document."

"*Mon cher ami*. Of course you would. I would not have suffered for hours in the back of that taxi if I didn't want you to meet Henri and his lovely wife Cherie."

As they all talked and ate their food, Pharrell's mind drifted momentarily. Angelique had not phoned him for days. Did she have feelings for him, he wondered? He saw the intimacy between Henri and Cherie and this reminded him of what perhaps was missing in his life.

The occasional silence in the conversation was broken only by the barks of the Rottweiler's patrolling the garden. "We feel safer with the dogs now. After the burglary we decided to get the Rottweiler's for protection. When you live in a secluded environment thieves think you are an easy target. At least, now, we have Jac and Jon our lovely dogs to protect us," Henri said.

"They certainly scared me…I don't know about Hugo, but those dogs gave me a fright and I would think any prospective thief will think twice," Pharrell exclaimed.

"I certainly hope you are right. Now, we have the dogs I feel a lot safer sleeping here. If I had my way I would replace Henri for Jac and Jon. At least the dogs don't snore," Cherie said laughing.

"They call it the *'Gateway to Heaven'*," Henri announced, changing the subject while slurping wine from a cut glass goblet.

"The gateway to heaven…that is what they called ancient Babylon. The city of the Gods is another name Babylon is known by. It's all about legends and myths," Henri said.

"Why is Babylon called the gateway to heaven?" Pharrell asked intently.

"That is a good question, Pharrell…and difficult to answer," Henri replied.

"Some say…it's just a legend. But, there is always a bit of truth in most legends. The Babylonians you could say created monotheism. They worshipped one God they called Marduk. The Jews that were in exile in Babylon and eventually returned to Israel continued the tradition of monotheism with their God Yahweh. You see…before the exile, the Jews adorned and worshipped numerous deities. The principle of monotheism was a new way to practice a religion at that time."

Cherie interrupting said, "The practice was so new to the Jews of Babylon…and don't forget they had been in captivity in Babylon for several generations. So, for many of them, the practice of worshipping one God was normal. It was something they saw every day."

"But, why is Babylon called the gateway to heaven?" Pharrell asked again.

"Babylon is famous for the hanging gardens of Babel. A structure built with many floors like a tower apartment block. At that time structures of this nature would have been rare…and would have been a marvel to see. To a visitor from outside Babylon these structures would have appeared to reach the clouds, and, therefore, likely to create the notion for many that indeed Babylon was the gateway to heaven. A legend or myth is then created around those assumptions and repeated from generation to generation," Henri replied.

"I understand what you are trying to say."

Henri continued talking, "Before the Babylonians the Sumerians who we understand from the cuneiform clay tablets that have been found in that part of the world were masters of reading the stars. It is said that they were the first astrologers. The Sumerian's invented the zodiac that we use today to predict events associated with the movement of planets and the stars. History has decided to call this region the cradle of civilisation or the dawn of civilisation because we know of no other part of the world as advanced at this time…around five thousand years ago. In this region farming took place on the fertile land between the river Tigress and the river Euphrates."

"You can easily see how legends and myths are born from such a rich history as ancient Babylon and Sumerian," Cherie said.

"So, what do you think about the legend of *Shahbla el Allah*?" Pharrell asked.

Cherie replied, "All legends have some truth. So, it's possible it did exist at some point in time. The problem becomes…where do you start?"

Hugo interrupted, "I have been telling Pharrell the same since he told me about his quest."

Henri replied, "Cherie is right…where do you start? It's like a puzzle with many missing pieces. It's a difficult task without all the clues. And then you are not sure exactly what you are looking for because the *Shahbla el Allah*, perhaps, has nothing to do with God but an entirely different subject altogether. Just how do you know when you have found it?"

Cherie said, "Your quest is similar to one of the lost books of the Bible. They discovered the book of Enoch when they found the Dead Sea Scrolls some years ago. Scholars knew of its existence, but without a copy they were in the dark as to what the book of Enoch was about. You have a legend about the *Shahbla el Allah* and not much else to go on, so your task is equally difficult, but an interesting quest. And I repeat what Henri said, just how do you know when you have found it?"

Everyone looked at Pharrell for his response. His face had turned red from blushing as he felt under pressure from the questioning. Breaking the silence he said, "Everything you have said makes sense. But it would not be a quest worth chasing if it was easy to unravel. Besides, I like a challenge and you just never know what you find along the way." The last sentenced triggered his thoughts about Angelique and briefly he felt comfortable under the spot light.

Hugo interrupted, "It's getting late…we need to get a taxi to the train station."

"No need. I will drive you to the train station. The dogs will guard the house while Cherie and I drive you to the station."

Hugo said, "Great, that's all settled then. Only wish we could have stayed longer, but we have to get back to Paris. I have an appointment with the Louvre tomorrow."

As they travelled to Hesdin train station about an hour's drive from Agincourt Henri spoke about the history of Agincourt. Hugo and Pharrell listened intently to what was said and individually decided not to interrupt Henri. Occasionally, Cherie added to Henri's history lesson as she drove through the countryside toward the station.

Suddenly, Cherie announced, "There on the left is where the battle took place between the English and French."

Hugo and Pharrell looked at the field; it looked to them as unremarkable as any other field in the surrounding countryside.

"So, this is where the battle of Agincourt took place," Pharrell muttered.

Henri and Cherie explained that the battle of Agincourt took place near the modern day town called *Azincourt* on St Crispin's Day in 1415 about 200Km from the port of Calais in the north-eastern part of France. For many

French people the battle between the English Henry V's army of around 10,000 men and the French King Charles VI army of around 30,000 men proved to be a significant turning point in French history, even though the French lost the battle for several reasons. The battle took place on a narrow strip of land bordered by thick forest on either side forcing the French men-at-arms who were heavy with body armour to wade through and cross several hundred metres of deep mud to reach the English lines and at the same time avoid the hail of arrows coming at them from each side of the English front line. The French cavalry also could not easily wade through the deep mud and attack the English archers who were protected on each side and into their adjacent forest with sharpened pointed wooden stakes driven into the ground. With so many horses and men-at-arms forced into a funnel the French suffered around ten times the casualties. Eventually, the French fled the battlefield having seen what had happened to their comrades. With so many dead noblemen the French aristocracy had been decimated giving rise for Joan of Arc to rally the French a few years later to effectively regain the parts of France previously controlled by the English crown. For the French people the battle of Agincourt gave rise for the unification of France under one French monarch.

Hugo said," The only reason why the English won the battle is because they had a secret weapon."

Pharrell asked curiously, "What was that?"

"Later…I will explain. *Mon cher*."

As they pulled into the train station the throng of people waiting was an unexpected site. Pharrell and Hugo said their good-byes and thanked Henri and Cherie for the lift and Hugo promised to keep in touch. They waved good-bye and turned into the station to buy their tickets to Paris. The lengthy queue to buy tickets they both realised was due to the national holiday and Bastille Day had brought many tourists and French nationals to visit Agincourt for the day. As the train approached there was a scurry of people eager to board the train first. Hugo and Pharrell felt lucky to find seats together amongst the scramble to board the train to Paris.

Hugo said, "We were fortunate to find these seats."

"Especially, today, Hugo. I would guess that a provincial station is normally not that busy, except for some tourists out for a day trip on a national holiday."

"Yes, *mon cher ami*. What did you think about Henri and Cherie?"

"What do you mean?"

"Well, I sensed they were holding back. What I mean is…they knew something, but were not saying for some reason."

"Hugo, I think you are just getting agitated because you have invested a huge sum of money in purchasing the papyri and you don't like any criticism. After all, they are your friends, and friends should be open about what they think."

Hugo asked inquisitively, "Are you honest with me?"

Pharrell annoyed at the question replied, "Of course, but sometimes friends need to ask difficult questions and remove the clouds of your judgements. Otherwise, you are likely to fall faster than a speeding bullet."

"Thanks. *Mon cher ami*. I guess you are right."

Pharrell decided to change the subject of the conversation. He already felt the pain inside. As he observed from where he sat a family enjoying the journey it reminded him of something he had never had. Did Angelique think the same as he did, he said to himself.

"What was the secret weapon at Agincourt?" Pharrell asked inquisitively eager to learn more like a school child intently listening to their school teacher.

"Oh yes…the battle of Agincourt. Henry the fifth was out numbered three to one against the French that day. But, Henry the fifth lined up his forces in such a way to force the French to attack funnelled in the centre opposite a bog. As the French knights on horseback charged they got stuck in the bog and then Henry unleashed his archers…the long bow. It was a slaughter…the long bow archers cut down the French cavalry with ease. As the battle raged many of the French soldiers panicked and fled because of the deadly long bow. The long bow was the secret weapon because it took many years of practice for the archers to gain the strength needed to pull the bow effectively. Every peasant and farmer had to learn to use the long bow from childhood…it was a decree from the King and had to be obeyed. The long bow archers were feared for many years until of course gun powder came along."

As Hugo continued talking Pharrell's eyes began to sag and the last thing he could remember was the face of the young boy sat opposite him on the train.

***

As the train entered the outskirts of Paris many of the passengers had started to stir and make their arrangements to leave. "Wake up…wake up Pharrell," Hugo said at the same time giving Pharrell a generous nudge.

"We are near our destination…Nord du Paris."

"How long have I been asleep?" Pharrell asked while trying to refocus his eyes to the lights of the train.

"Most of the way you have been snoring. And I've had to give you a nudge here and there."

"I've been dreaming, Hugo."
"You can tell me later…we get off here," Hugo replied while coveting the safety of their hotel. "I need a drink and some food."
"Tomorrow…is a big day. We have a meeting at the Louvre," Hugo said to Pharrell as they sat in the taxi approaching their hotel.
"I thought you said tonight to Henri and Cherie?"
"Yes and no…*mon cher*. Tomorrow we have an appointment with the contact Lucy Bouchard gave us. But tonight we can visit the Louvre as tourists." Hugo replied candidly.
"We can stay around the hotel if you wish," Hugo said as their taxi pulled up outside the entrance to their hotel. The neon light gave a welcome entrance and Hugo safely stored the papyri in the hotel's safe for the night.
"The dream you had earlier…was it pleasurable?" Hugo asked as they sat and enjoyed the fine cuisine and wines their hotel had to offer. From where Pharrell sat he could observe the young couple briefly holding hands inconspicuously dining in the corner of the dining room. The couple were in love. He could see their affection with each other and he wanted the same desire, he thought.
"Yes and no," Pharrell replied with the same word game Hugo played. His thoughts were of Angelique. He felt the pangs of desire. But he was not about to reveal to Hugo how he really felt. Not right now, he said to himself before answering Hugo.
"Have you heard from Angelique?" Hugo asked while slurping down some wine.
It was like he could read his mind. His thoughts were of Angelique. Why had she not phoned him?
"No not today, Hugo."

Pharrell was lying and decided to change the subject of conversation. "What was the name of the contact at the Louvre?"

"Michel Napier."

"Lucy said he is the director of Egyptian Antiquities and specialises in conserving papyrus. Hopefully, we can hook another fish, *mon ami*."

"Do you want me to take the lead in negotiations tomorrow?" Pharrell asked while watching Hugo stroking his beard thinking of a reply. "No, we will play this one as a team. Because I think we have a stronger hand as a pair. Besides, I don't think they will buy the papyri…not right now anyway."

"What are we seeing him for?" Pharrell asked exasperated.

"Because if I know that Jew Harry Lebervitz…the idea of someone else interested in buying the papyri will…as you say…grease the deal. Harry probably already knows our contact at the Louvre. I would not be surprised if Harry had someone following us since the day we saw him. He's that type of dealer…covers all angles…so to speak," Hugo replied.

***

The following day Pharrell and Hugo made their way to the Louvre. It was surprisingly busy with a long queue of noisy school children waiting to enter after Bastille Day. The phone call Hugo had made to Michel Napier at the Louvre in the taxi moments earlier had certainly avoided the need to queue.

Michel Napier was a middle-age man with a comb over uselessly trying to cover his balding head and wearing thick rimmed spectacles. He greeted Pharrell and Hugo cordially with a welcome hand shake and ushered them into a nearby room away from the noise of the crowd outside in the main reception area. As they took their seats around a large antique table Pharrell noticed the surveillance camera peering down at them from the corner of the ceiling. Perhaps, they don't trust their employees, he said to himself.

"Now, Lucy Bouchard informs me that you have some interesting papyri to evaluate. Can I see it, please?" Michel Napier asked politely.

"Yes, of course," Hugo replied while handing over the leather binder containing the papyri.

As Michel Napier inspected the papyri Pharrell and Hugo stayed silent. Pharrell watched as each papyrus were read in turn as the man occasionally glanced above his spectacles at him and Hugo before continuing his examination. Pharrell pondered what the man perhaps was thinking. Did he believe it was genuine as they did?

"Yes, an interesting legend is recorded on these papyruses. The land of ancient Mesopotamian has always fascinated me. Did you know that the first known civilisation started in this region between the Euphrates River in the west and the Tigress River in the east?" Michel Napier continued his history lesson without waiting for a reply with only a brief pause to check if his captive audience were listening to him. "The regular flooding of the two rivers provided a rich abundance of fertile soils to cultivate crops for the early settlers. The early settlers were originally hunter gatherers who became sophisticated farmers."

Pharrell asked curiously, "Around what time in history did this take place?"

"It's difficult to say an exact time in history, because history is constantly being reassessed. But, about five thousand years B.C early settlers had formed communities and villages and some of these eventually became cities supporting perhaps several tens of thousands of people."

"We know these people as the ancient Sumerians, and as you probably know they invented a written language amongst many great achievements for this time in history," Michel said.

Pharrell and Hugo just sat there and patiently listened to the expert as he clearly rivalled in imparting his wealth of information. Michel Napier was in his element; he often gave lectures to school children and today was no different as far as he was concerned. Pausing briefly to adjust his spectacles he continued his lecture.

"We know a lot about the Sumerian's because of the wealth of written information preserved on clay tablets. When the legendary capital of the Sumer called Ur was found in what is now part of southern Iraq in the early nineteenth century, when they excavated the site, they found several thousand of these clay tablets. And, after decoding the cuneiform inscriptions archaeologists have been able to piece together how the ancient Sumerians lived."

Pharrell decided he needed to know what if anything the man knew about his quest. He wanted the facts and not a history lesson even though he was intrigued by what the man had to say. He also saw how impatient Hugo looked as he kept silent waiting for the man to pronounce on his investment. Did the man believe the *Shahbla el Allah* was just a legend or myth or a genuine artefact as he did, he mused? "What do you know about the legendary book of God referred to in the papyri?"

"I did wonder if you would ask me that question. And the answer is I don't know. What I mean is…Yes, I believe in the legend and so do many other scholars.

The proof of that are your papyri. But, like other references to the *Shahbla el Allah* we don't know what the book was about. We can only assume and make wild speculation as to its contents," Michel replied.

Pharrell and Hugo were getting impatient, with Hugo sweating more as each minute passed and Pharrell aware that Michel knew more about his quest than he was prepared to say. Perhaps, Michel was like him a latent explorer and adventurer or a grave digger, Pharrell said to himself as a wry smile crept across his face.

"Anyway, I have been talking about the Sumerians and not the Babylonians whom came after the Sumerians."

"Yes, I know...but could the *Shahbla el Allah* exist written in Greek or Aramaic somewhere?" Pharrell asked intently.

"Yes, but again unless it actually states it's the *Shahbla el Allah* then how would you know? Whoever or whenever a legend is created it becomes known by that name, but it probably started out totally different and over many years the legend is told, it then gets corrupted until it differs completely from its original state."

Pharrell exasperated asked, "Could you offer a clue as to what you think it may have been?"

"The Babylonians worshipped many Gods, but the most important one we believe was Marduk who apparently lived at the top of a stepped shape structure called a ziggurat, many examples of this type of construction can be seen today in different parts of the Middle East. The Babylonians followed a strict procedure when they made offerings to Marduk and when they built a new building they buried effigies of their God under the foundations to sanctify and bring good omens. So, your answer is Marduk."

Pharrell noticed the sweat appearing on Hugo's brow after waiting in silence for so long in a room without windows in the middle of summer. Hugo looked like a man under pressure to him, as each minute passed in silence with only the occasional murmur from him as the man from the Louvre continued deciding the fate of Hugo's huge investment. The longer the silence it was a good sign even if it took its toll on Hugo.

"Can I take one of the papyruses out for closer inspection?" Michel asked.

"Yes, of course," Hugo replied.

Michel Napier carefully teased out the papyrus from the clear plastic folder onto a large sheet of paper. Placing the papyrus under the light of the desk lamp he carefully examined each section minutely before revealing his thoughts. "I understand you have sent samples for carbon dating," he said.

At last the man was asking questions, he said to himself, before answering. Lucy certainly informed him, that was only to be expected, he thought. "Yes, it will be a few days, perhaps a week before we receive the results," Hugo replied.

"Fine, Lucy Bouchard has told me you would like to sell the papyri to the museum. Providing the carbon dating results are consistent with the era then I would present your papyri to one of our purchasing committees, which oversea this kind of investment. We would also conduct a comprehensive analysis before deciding on a purchase. This procedure could take several weeks or even months before a final decision. Would this be acceptable to you?"

"Yes, of course," Hugo replied.

"Oh, what is your asking price," Michel asked.

"One million dollars is my asking price." Hugo replied curtly knowing that any purchase by the museum would eventually depend on many factors, not least, other interested parties, especially, another high profile museum like the New York Guggenheim. It was a good idea to start with a high figure to negotiate with, that way he had some margin for bargaining, he surmised.

"Ok, that's it for today. Please, let me know when you have the carbon dating results and how you want to precede from there," Michel Napier said.

Hugo was mystified and more than disappointed from the lengthy examination at the Louvre by Michel Napier. He was expecting a clearer indication of the authenticity of papyri from this expert.

Hugo asked, "I thought you would have given your expert view on the authenticity of the papyri today, Mr. Napier."

"Mr. Deschamps my job here is not to give valuations or decide if items are genuine or not, that process as I mentioned before is for one of our committees."

"But, surely you have an opinion you could offer to me, today?" Hugo asked. Pharrell saw the sweat roll down Hugo's face as he quizzed Napier for more information. He realised the huge investment Hugo had made purchasing the papyri had started to affect him. Just how much stress this investment had put on Hugo was anyone's guess.

"Ok, because of your friendship with Lucy Bouchard, and, as a favour for you I will tell you what I think. First, you must appreciate that my appraisal is not binding and is not binding in anyway on the museum. Is that understood?"

"Yes, I understand Mr. Napier," Hugo said eagerly.

"The papyri have the feel of a genuine article and the language used is contemporary with the period. So, without carbon dating and ink testing a final conclusion cannot be made. That is all I can say at the moment, Mr Deschamps." Michel Napier said.

Hugo looked at Pharrell with a look of relief on his face. Pharrell seized the moment to ask Napier if he could contact him about his quest in the future.

"You can always contact me here, Mr Anderson," Napier tersely replied.

Mr Napier shook hands with them both and escorted them to the main entrance of the Louvre. Pharrell and Hugo noticed the queues were just as long as before.

"At least, we didn't have to queue Hugo," Pharrell remarked.

"Let's get back to the hotel. I need a shower and a change of clothes after that boiler of a room. I think, I was nearly ready to pass out. The sweat just kept coming as we waited for Mr. Napier to pronounce judgement, like a court judge," Hugo jollily said.

Pharrell nodded with agreement and gave a smile at Hugo's remark. At least, the taxi ride back to their hotel allowed Hugo to cool off with the car window wound down allowing the rush of air to ease his sweating, even though he could taste the Parisian pollution as it swirled around the inside of the taxi, Pharrell mused.

***

"How was Thailand?" the editor asked.

"Tom, you always ask, the simplest of questions, before I have had time to file a report. So, the simple answer is great. Is that good enough?" Angelique replied amused.

"There's a section briefing in five minutes. I hope you are ready." Tom said smiling.

Angelique curtly smiled back at Tom and knew the procedure at the Federal Bureau of Investigation like she knew the back of her hand. After all she was no rooky at the job. Her role as an undercover agent meant she had to be prepared for any eventuality. She guessed Tom was just jealous of her role and he was probably bored of being a desk jockey, she thought.

The section head looked around the table at the men and women gathered for the briefing and before saying a word thought about the task ahead. Many years had passed since his days as a field agent, his time now required a different set of skills managing people, although there were times when the lure of his youth bothered him, he mused.

"Good morning…I hope everyone has read the latest memo," he said.

"I begin with an intro…This is agent Fabio Cacliticio from the C.I.A….He is assigned from today to liaise between the F.B.I. and the C.I.A. on this case. As you all know from time to time both agencies overlap and since nine eleven those in Washington D.C. require different government organisations to share information and more importantly to work together on cases that are of national interest."

"Before I continue are there any questions so far?" he asked.

"Yes…do we have the lead in all arrests and indictments?" one of the agents asked.

"Yes, the F.B.I. is the lead investigator in this case. But, it all depends how the case affects the national interest as who makes indictments. We don't want a turf war, so remember this is a joint investigation from today. All new information and case progress will be discussed at these briefings on a weekly basis for now. Any agent not present at these briefings is expected to alert the editor and to pass on any new information," the section head replied.

"Oh, by the way, Fabio that applies to you as well. The editor is Tom Jajivic who runs the cover operation here. Please, put your hand up Tom and introduce yourself to Fabio…I am sure you two will get on well working together."

Tom stood up and said hello before sitting down again to hear the progress of the case from the section head.

"At the moment we have several agents working under cover and one of them has just returned from Thailand. Please, introduce yourself to Fabio…Sarah and give us a briefing on your progress," the section head asked.

Sarah said hello to Fabio and immediately started briefing her colleagues without waiting for Fabio to react to her introduction. "The Thai mafia is shipping large amounts of counterfeit currency from Thailand to the Asia sub-continent in exchange for an array of different goods such as; rare artefacts, heroin, guns and stolen art work. The Thai mafia is using the border between Miramar and Thailand to move these goods because the ports in Miramar are an easy place to bribe port officials and dock workers without too much attention from the local police and government agencies. As you know Miramar formerly Burma was a closed society until recently and run by the Generals. And even though the country is trying to westernise itself Miramar still has a lot of corruption to deal with. I also have a target lead that I have been investigating that perhaps will provide us with some more information. All current information is provided in the report I submitted this morning. I am due to return to Thailand within the next few days to continue the investigation. Are there any questions?"

"How long have you been working undercover in Thailand?" Fabio asked intently.

"About six months. My cover name is Angelique Bergerhof. I work as a journalist for the Washington Inquirer and this building is its headquarters and Tom Jajivic is our editor. Our operation here is made legit by real journalists working for the F.B.I producing a monthly magazine with real stories. So, to the outside world we are a magazine enterprise this allows our agents cover to go anywhere in the world."

"Thank you, Sarah."

"Many of you here are probably wondering why the C.I.A are interested in this case." The section head caught sight of many of the faces gathered, to him some looked interested, but most had the look of agents who had spent too many years in the field and were ready to retire if they were offered the right severance package, he thought. "Sarah mentioned the Thai mafia were trading guns for currency. The C.I.A. believes some of these guns are ending up in the hands of terrorists. That is all I can say for the moment. So, if there are no more questions…the briefing is closed," the section head said.

As the briefing closed and people began leaving the section head asked Sarah to stay. "I want you to liaise with Fabio over the next few days before you return to Thailand. Is that okay," the section head asked.

"Yes, of course," Sarah replied.

"Fabio, this is one of our best agents…Sarah Milligan. She will fill you in on our operation here and coordinate intelligence between the F.B.I. and the C.I.A. while she is in Thailand until further notice. Is that understood, Sarah?" the section head asked.

"Yes, of course. Will you need a daily report or are you just interested in any intelligence concerning the gun smuggling, Fabio?" Sarah asked.

"Everything you find out, not just the gun smuggling," Fabio replied.

Sarah realised from Fabio's reply that the C.I.A. were interested in the F.B.I operation for more than they were saying. It was typical of the C.I.A. to keep its cards to its chest. Even though government security organisations since nine eleven were meant to work hand in hand in cooperation together with the C.I.A. they still operated on a need to know basis that meant sharing nothing of value.

She looked at the tall Italian looking man and decided she would have to bide her time before he was going to let her know what the real intentions of the C.I.A were, if he ever would. Perhaps, her feminine attractions would loosen his tongue, she mused. "Will you be joining me in Thailand," she asked Fabio.

"No, not at present unless you think I should at some point," he replied snappily.

Sarah smiled without answering and looked at her section chief to see his reaction to this interaction between them both. She suspected the C.I.A. was keeping back something from the F.B.I and she was determined to find out what if it was possible.

"Good, I can see you both are going to work together like a house on fire. It's always good to see a bit of friction between agents of different agencies, otherwise, a malaise can develop and we don't want that do we," the section chief remarked.

Fabio seized the moment as the section chief returned to his office. "Fancy a drink after work?" he said to Sarah as she was about to leave the briefing room.

She nodded her head and agreed to meet Fabio in the bar across the road from their building after work with the proviso that it would be a friendly drink and not a date. Although she was eager to find out from Fabio what the C.I.A's real interest was, she was not about to start a relationship with a working colleague, even though he was an attractive man, she said to herself.

***

"Let's get ready, *mon cher*, we have a date with Lucy at the University," Hugo said happily. Pharrell observed how Hugo had an extra spring in his movements that morning as he prepared himself in front of the mirror in their hotel room. His eagerness to get to Lucy's University was evident in the rush to have breakfast that normally took Hugo a considerable length of time.

The University of Paris was not how Pharrell imagined it would be as the taxi pulled up outside the main entrance. The University complex was a mixture of old and new buildings scattered over many acres. Luckily, Hugo's native tongue made it easy for him to follow directions. Pharrell observed the throng of students as ants piling into one building and exiting another as one great mad rush before the start of a lecture.

Lucy's office was situated in a part of one of the older buildings that had used hardwoods liberally to decorate the walls and floors in a time when cutting down trees in the Amazon was not an issue as it is today. Lucy's office was crammed with shelves of books and virtually all the space around her desk were piles of what looked like student's work ready and waiting to be marked.

After the customary hug and kiss on the cheeks Hugo and Pharrell sat down amongst the piles of paper and eagerly waited for the results of the carbon dating. She passed the report to Hugo and then outlined the main findings of the carbon dating.

"As you can see Hugo from the graph the carbon dating suggests a date approximately between five hundred B.C. and three hundred B.C. for the papyri. That is consistent with what I told you when you asked my opinion before the carbon dating," Lucy said.

"That's great...this is the news I have been waiting for," Hugo roared.

"Hold on Hugo...Wait, I haven't finished yet, be patient," she said.

"The tests on the ink samples are not so conclusive. There are some inconsistencies with the ink tests."

"What do you mean," Hugo asked impatiently.

"Some of the ink samples do correspond with the same time frame, but one sample has a carbon dating that has a time frame about five hundred years later which would be around the time of the birth of Christ...Give or take one hundred years or so. This could mean many things such as some of the papyrus text was later added because a scribe has added text at a later date or the sample was corrupted somehow.

"What do you think," Hugo asked curiously.

"Most likely, a scribe at some point has added text to one of the papyruses. This was common practice, at this time, because of the scarcity of writing materials, so scribes would rub out or wash the papyrus removing the previous text so that new text could be added to the papyrus. I believe this is what has happened in this case," Lucy replied.

"This sounds interesting and perhaps intriguing," Hugo said.

"Tests have shown that it is the fourth piece or page of the papyri that the carbon dating of the ink used is around five hundred years later. We can if you wish use a process called ultra-violet spectrographic analysis to reveal the hidden writing on the papyrus. Would you like to do that...It may take a week before we have the results?" Lucy asked.

Hugo thought for a while, he knew his potential buyers would what to know what the hidden writing revealed and so did he. "Okay, Lucy go ahead and make the arrangements, I will head back to the hotel and fetch the papyrus from the safe."

Pharrell felt unwanted at this one sided conversation between the two of them. "I will come with you, Hugo. I have forgotten my mobile," he said, awkwardly trying to avoid eye contact with Lucy.

In the taxi Hugo expressed his glee at the good news about the papyri. And apologized to Pharrell about the amount of time the sale of the papyri was taking. "No need to apologize, Hugo…I understand the pressure this sale has caused you. I have not heard from Angelique for several days now and perhaps I was leaping ahead of myself."

"Perhaps, she tried and the mobile roaming service hasn't worked," Hugo said.

"Perhaps…," he replied to Hugo while not bothering to finish the sentence.

Hugo decided to change the subject of conversation; he could see the sorrow in Pharrell's eyes at the disappointment of not hearing from Angelique. "Did you see that blue Citroen parked just down the road from Lucy's house? It pulled out when we turned into the main road and has been following us."

"No, I didn't…But then again I have not been looking," Pharrell replied.

"Not to worry Pharrell, I believe we have been followed for several days now. Most likely Harry Lebervitz has had us tailed for several days. I told you that old dog would do something like that."

"Are you sure it's his doing and not someone else?" Pharrell asked.

"Yes, most likely…Who else could it be?" Hugo replied not expecting a reply to his question.

As Pharrell waited in the taxi outside their hotel for Hugo to return with the papyri, he caught a glance through the driver's rear mirror of a blue Citroen parked about a hundred metres up the road. He decided not to turn around, but would watch what the car did as they returned to Lucy's home. Perhaps, Hugo was right, they had been followed, and Pharrell decided he would wait and see what happened.

"You're right, Hugo, we are being followed," Pharrell announced to Hugo.

"Yes, I saw the car when I got into the taxi. Don't mention this to Lucy it will only make her worried. It safe to say this is Harry's work. That old Jew is only protecting his future investment. I remember years ago when I was negotiating a first edition of '1984' by George Orwell, he had me followed for days. For days I wasn't sure if I was being followed until one day I decided to get rid of my tail. Luckily, I was able to lose my tail and follow him, which led me back to Harry's office. From that moment, I realised that Harry was only protecting his investment. I guess he wanted to know the competitors and of course what the sellers were up to. It's his calling card…And, it must be profitable because he works for all the major museums and galleries in America."

"Are you sure it's Harry's work and not someone else?" Pharrell asked startled.

"Don't worry Pharrell, I am certain its Harry's work…We have nothing to be worried about. From what I know about Harry he is shrewd and careful with his money, but, he is not the sort of person to hurt you in any way. To him, it's just business. And for us it helps to grease the deal…The more he knows about whom we see the more likely it is he will be jealous of the prospect of other competitors. Harry will not want an auction; he'll want to negotiate on his terms and with the knowledge of possibly competitors in the background."

Hugo and Pharrell could see Lucy waiting by the front door as the taxi pulled up outside. Hugo handed Lucy the papyri and Hugo expressed the importance to Lucy of a speedy result of the spectrograph analysis. Lucy promised Hugo the results of the spectrograph within a few days and suggested all three of them meet for a night out in Paris the following night.

As Hugo and Pharrell's taxi turned into main road both of them caught sight of the blue car parked up the road. The blue Citroën continued to follow their taxi all the way back to their hotel.

***

"Hello, Mr. Lebervitz. It's Jac…. "

"Yes, what do you have for me?" Impatiently, Harry grunted.

"Yesterday, Hugo and Pharrell visited Lucy Bouchard a professor at the University of Paris. Apparently, she is an expert in ancient linguistics, especially, Greek and Aramaic. Following that visit Hugo and Pharrell took a taxi to Agincourt to the home of Henri and Cherie Piccar. Henri Piccar is a well-known author whom specialises in historical nonfiction and fiction. Then, they took the train back to Paris and then I assume back to their hotel."

"So, you are not sure what they did after they returned to Paris?" Harry asked interrupting Jac with anger in the tone of his voice.

"No, it's difficult to follow when they changed their mode of transport," Jac replied trying to keep his composure under pressure from Harry's obvious annoyance at his failure to follow Hugo and Pharrell onto the train.

Jac continued his verbal report, "The following day they visited the Louvre and saw Michel Napier who is a director of antiquities. Throughout these visits Hugo carried a leather folder."

"This Michel Napier, what else do you know about him?"

"Not much…Not had enough time to find out. The information I have is that he's an expert on ancient papyrus."

"Oh, that's interesting. Try to find out if the Louvre is interested in what Hugo and Pharrell are selling. Okay?"

"Okay, but do you know what they are selling?" Jac asked.

"Yes, of course, but I want to know if the Louvre are interested. Do you understand?" Harry said impatiently.

Jac realised Harry was hiding something, and that something probably involved a lot of money. He wanted to know, so perhaps he could find a way to extract more money from this case, he surmised.

"Okay, Mr Lebervitz. I will be in touch…" Jac said, as the phone went dead.

***

Lucy was waiting by the front door of her home as they pulled up in the taxi. Hugo had promised an interesting night as they made their way into the centre of Paris. The lights of the Eiffel Tower glistened in the darkness as the taxi drove through the Arc de Triomphe amongst the chaos of the evening traffic. The night club was busy, but luckily they found a table and ordered their drinks amongst the frenzied sounds of the jazz band playing and the noise of people in deep *tête-à-tête*.

"Have you been here before, Hugo?" Lucy asked curiously.

"Yes, many times in the past." Hugo had to raise the tone of his voice above the sound of the jazz band just to be heard. "I like it because you can have a conversation but at the same time listen to the music," Hugo explained.

"I believe you're right," Pharrell agreed.

"I see some people are dancing over there, fancy a dance Pharrell?" Lucy asked intently.

"Yes, why not…It's night to let loose and enjoy ourselves."

"You go ahead…perhaps, when I've had a few more drinks I will join you," Hugo remarked.

When the music slowed his embrace of Lucy in his arms triggered his hormones and he felt his erection growing. He was sure Lucy could feel his erection as he held her close to his body. He was embarrassed at how his body reacted to Lucy's charms, but she was very attractive for an older woman, he mused.

"Do you find me attractive?" she asked.

Pharrell was startled at the direct question at first, but then realised his erection must have been a wakeup call.

"Yes, you are very attractive. What were you expecting me to say?" Pharrell quizzed her back.

"Would you like to make love with me?" she asked.

Pharrell took several seconds before replying. "No, I am already taken, but it's a nice offer."

"Okay, let's get back to Hugo," she abruptly replied.

Pharrell realised Lucy's feathers had been ruffled at this refusal. It was his over active erection giving the primordial urge, without consideration about how he felt about Angelique. He loved Angelique, he whispered to himself.

"This place is famous for some of its patrons," Hugo announced.

"The French actor Gérard Depardieu was a frequent patron and the great Ernest Hemingway apparently used the night club in nineteen twenties to meet many of his friends here such as; Scott Fitzgerald and his wife Zelda. Hemingway wrote about his passion for Paris in his little known tome called 'A Moveable Feast,' and that reminds me are you hungry?"

"I know a great place to eat that has the finest cuisine at affordable prices," Hugo said.

"Yes, that sounds good," Pharrell agreed.

"What have you in mind, Hugo?" Lucy asked curiously.

"The *Aviation Club de France Casino* on the *Champs-Elysées*, not far from the *Arc d'Triomphe*," Hugo replied.

"I didn't think you gambled, Hugo?"

"I don't, but this casino produces some of the best food you can eat at this time of night. Believe me; you will thank me after you have tasted their cuisine and you can also have as many America cocktails as you can think of."

"What do you say, Lucy?"

"Yes, okay with me. Let's finish our drinks and make our way," Lucy replied.

Hugo agreed without thinking, his mind was elsewhere. He wanted to quickly scan the room for someone out of place. He was looking for a loner, who looked like a fish out of water. At most of the tables he saw couples with friends busily chatting and watching the band, and there at the back of the bar with a clear view of his table, he saw a well-built, mid-thirties man with dark skin features sat alone drinking. He could not see how tall he was, but his physique suggested he was a giant. He had caught a glimpse of him, and that was enough, was this Harry's man, who had been tailing him and Pharrell. He had to be sure, at the casino he would know for sure, he said to himself. His previous encounter with Harry Lebervitz had taught him what to look for; he would be a loner, who looked like a fish out of water, he mused.

"Yes, let's go...," Hugo said, as they walked out of the bar. Hugo was able to have another glimpse of the man's features and what he was wearing without looking directly at him from the corner of his left eye. He decided not worry Lucy and Pharrell about the man who perhaps was following them. It would only frighten and alarm them, he thought.

"Good evening," the doorman said.

The casino was busy as usual thought Hugo, especially this time of night when most night clubs are about to close for the night, and, it's the only game into town where you can continue drinking to the early hours of the morning. Then there are those; the gamblers who spend all day and night at the casino trying to win back their losses, but, end up deeper into debt. Then there are the lucky ones; who arrive for the first time at the casino and win and win, as if lucky luck has smiled on them, and no matter what game they played they ended up winning. Then there are the stooges, who hang around waiting for a rich patron to favour them or the table becomes hot and they place their money accordingly. Then there are the drinkers, loners, and anybody else who had decided they have nowhere else to go but to the casino. Then of course there are the girls or women who seek the frill of a big spender willing to favour their charms. And last of all are the employees who have their hand out at every opportunity to gleefully grasp what they can before you lose it all to the casino.

"Let's head for the restaurant and find a table," Hugo announced.

"I have an appetite for some fine French cuisine," Pharrell said.

"I do too," Lucy agreed.

They ordered their food and drinks above the distant sound of fruit machines ringing and croupiers announcing winning numbers and cards. Pharrell imagined coins tumbling down the fruit machines from his memory of seaside piers. As a child his parents would take him to visit Oslo on the coast in Norway and they would spend their money trying to win a soft toy in the penny arcades. "Do you gamble much…Hugo?" Pharrell asked sheepishly.

"Every day, *mon cher*," Hugo replied smiling.

"What do you mean, Hugo?" Lucy asked keenly.

"You see, every time I invest in a book, a document or an artefact I know I could lose my money, but it's a gamble, and hopefully, with the odds in my favour," Hugo replied grinning like a Cheshire cat.

"That makes you a gambler as well, Pharrell," said Hugo. Hugo drew his attention briefly from Lucy and Pharrell and quickly scanned the restaurant, without Lucy and Pharrell noticing. The man that perhaps was following them was not in the restaurant. He expected the man was in the bar, probably a drinker, he surmised.

"*Voulez-vous rien d'autre*, Monsieur," the waiter said bowing and probably thinking about the tip this trio perhaps would give him, Hugo mused.

"*Merci...*," Hugo replied, gesturing with his hands that he was pleased with the waiter. He momentarily, thought, about the journey from the jazz bar to the casino. He could only see the bright lights of other cars through the rear mirror of the taxi. The blue Citroën was nowhere to be seen.

"Are you pleased with the carbon dating results, Hugo," Lucy asked, while reclining back in her seat sipping on a fine Beaujolai red wine. Eagerly anticipating Hugo's reply with a broad blushing red facial complexion caused by too much red wine.

"Yes and no. I'm intrigued to know what the spectrograph will reveal. But at the same time I would like to sell the papyri as soon as possible," Hugo replied.

"Why?" Lucy asked interrupting Pharrell's chance to join the conversation.

"Also, I would like to return to Thailand, my girlfriend Ning is worried about me," Hugo replied abruptly without thinking about Lucy's feelings.

Pharrell agreed, "Me, too."

Lucy nodded her head in agreement with Pharrell's and Hugo's remarks. Without revealing her bruised sensibilities, she then smiled at both of them. But, inside, her emotions had been bruised, although she was careful not to reveal what she felt.

"Did you know that the Thai's don't have casinos? The only form of gambling allowed in Thailand is their national lottery, "Hugo remarked.

"A good thing," Lucy agreed.

"Yes, I agree," Pharrell felt the same.

Hugo nodded his head in agreement and had another quick glance around the restaurant. He felt sure that Harry's man would be somewhere in the casino. "Do you know the story about the man who broke the bank of Monte Carlo?"

Pharrell and Lucy waited in anticipation for Hugo to tell his story. Pharrell had noticed Hugo's brief glance around the restaurant and wondered if Hugo was looking for someone, he surmised that Hugo was looking for the person driving the blue Citroën that had been following them.

Hugo said, "Well, the man who broke the bank of Monte Carlo…The story goes that one night in the world famous casino at Monte Carlo a rare event happened. On this particular night a series of blacks kept on appearing on the roulette wheel. In fact, a series of thirty three blacks in a row. Now, all this time nearly everyone except a few shrewd patrons continued to bet red in the hope that a red would soon appear. Of course, it didn't for thirty three times and the house, that is the casino made a fortune from the patrons backing against black. The story goes that one man kept his money on black, and, each time it doubled his stake, he quickly reached the casino limit, which was probably several million. You see the power of two in mathematics means that you only need to double your stake each time to the power of sixteen before you have hit a million. So, if the man was allowed to continue betting on black, he would have indeed broken the bank provided he stopped before a red turned up on the roulette wheel. In this story, at least, the man walked away a rich man, and the casino made a lot of money as well."

"Is this a true story or one of your tales?" Pharrell asked awkwardly.

"It's a true story…Black did appear for thirty three times in a row. I'm not sure about the date; I believe it happened in the nineteen sixties. Nobody knows the man's name that walked away with millions because he was never seen again at the casino. I guess the man wanted to remain anonymous."

"With that sort of money…most people would want anonymity," Lucy remarked.

Hugo was keen to know if the man that had been following them was in the casino bar. "Let's go down to the bar and watch what's happening on the casino floor." He wanted to get a better picture of his face.

As they entered the bar Hugo quickly recognized the bulky features of the man he suspected was following them, the loner that stuck out like a sore thumb. In the lights of the casino bar he saw the man's face, it was same man that had been tailing them, there was no mistake he was like a Hercules compared to other patrons sat around the bar drinking and he was alone amongst the crowd.

The waiter asked, "*Voulez-Vous?*"

They ordered some drinks as the trio found a table overlooking the casino and sat down. Hugo could see the man at a distance near the exit at the back of the bar; he was now sure he was the man that had been following them. The glimpse he had of the man's face under the lights of the bar was enough to convince him that it was Harry's man. Possibly an ex-soldier of Corsican descent, the French army recruit many of its soldiers from Corsica because of their fighting spirit, he mused.

"Are you going to try your luck at the tables, Hugo?" Lucy asked.

"I don't need luck, Lucy," Hugo replied laughing.

Pharrell asked, "Isn't all games of chance a matter of luck?"

Lucy agreed, "Yes, you need luck to win."

"Yes, you need luck sometimes in anything you do, but there is such a thing as the law of favourability. When someone does something for the first time they usually end up winning...they call this the law of favourability. It lets you believe it's easy and then sucks you in," Hugo said.

"Yes, they call it beginners luck," Pharrell exclaimed.

"Yes, that's right Pharrell. You see...The laws of the universe are defined in mathematics and odds are stacked against you on any game you play in the casino."

"I thought you can win at Blackjack if you can count the cards?" Lucy asked amenably as she decided she would test the law of favourability before it was time to leave. She wanted to test Hugo's theory for herself.

"Yes, you can, but it's illegal to count cards and besides you need a large bankroll to even out the variance." Hugo announced while catching another glimpse of Harry's man at the bar.

"What do you mean...variance?" Lucy asked intently.

"Take a look at the casino floor, you will see no poker tables those games are usually played in a side room where the casino take a small percentage of the winning pot called the rake. Whereas, all games on the casino floor you are playing against the house...the casino, and when you play poker you are playing against the skills of the other poker players. A good poker player knows that to make a steady profit you need to even out the variance by playing several poker tables at the same time...they do this by means of the internet. Because even a skilled poker player will have bad cards, but over several tables the variance of bad or good luck will even out and the good poker player will make a living. Now, do you understand variance?" Hugo asked.

"Yes, but how does that apply to the casino games," Pharrell asked.

"Because they are all fixed odds, and the longer you play them the more likely the casino will take your money. When you play poker you are playing against other poker players and not the fixed odds of the casino, so variance becomes a major part of a poker game."

"Yes, I see what you mean, Hugo," Pharrell said.

"Me, too," Lucy agreed.

Pharrell decided to change the conversation. He wanted to know what Lucy knew about his quest. He saw how Lucy had become more lucid as the evening rolled on into the early hours of the following day. "Lucy, tell me everything you know about the legend of the Shahbla *el Allah*?"

"You asked before, and, I told you unless you fancy yourself as a gravedigger…you'll have to wait for another *Dead Sea Scrolls*," Lucy replied, laughing at her own joke, but aware how it embarrassed Pharrell.

"Yes, I like your joke, but there must be something. Think, perhaps, a place, a person or an ancient text, which I can research? Pharrell asked smiling hoping that his open agreement with Lucy's joke would reveal a clue he could follow.

"St. Anthony's Monastery, the oldest ancient Christian abbey in the Egyptian desert, you could try there because they have a large library of early books that date from around the first and second century A.D. And, also Sheik Abul Adnin an Egyptian antiquities dealer, he perhaps will have some knowledge of your quest," Lucy replied.

"Have you any contact details for this Sheik Abul Adnin?" Pharrell asked.

"No, but ask around and you will find he is well known in the antiquities market in Egypt."

Pharrell felt pleased that he had squeezed some more information out of Lucy. She was like a lemon the more you squeezed the more juice came out. She probably knew more, but for some reason, she was holding back, he thought.

"Let's finish these drinks and head back home," Hugo announced.

"I would like to play the roulette wheel before we go," Lucy said.

"Okay, as long as you promise me, you can leave when I ask. Because when people gamble they make the mistake of chasing their losses," Hugo said.

"Place your bets," the croupier said.

Lucy decided she wanted to test Hugo's theory about beginners luck at the roulette wheel. She placed some of her chips on two numbers that meant something in her life.

"*vingt-quatre*," the croupier announced.

Lucy had won on the first spin of the roulette wheel. It was her lucky number twenty four, her son's birthday number. By placing most of her chips on this number, her winnings were considerable and she felt encouraged to continue.

"Now is the time to walk away," Hugo said to Pharrell as they watched Lucy placing her chips at the roulette table amongst a crowd of patrons trying to place their bets before the next spin. Hugo watched the anticipation of a win on Lucy's face and also the disappointment of losing. He had another quick glance at the bar and saw that Harry's man had gone, he probably realised he had seen enough for the night and went home and it was something they needed to do before Lucy lost her money.

"I have ordered a taxi," Hugo gently whispered into Lucy's ear.

"Okay, it's time to cash out," she replied.

Hugo was right about beginner's luck she thought as she exchanged her chips for cash. The money she had won she would spend on her son, she said to herself. In the taxi on their way home Lucy said to Hugo, "You were right about beginner's luck."

"Yes…It usually works out that way. But don't make the mistake of thinking you can repeat the experience," Hugo said.

"No…Hugo, but I did enjoy this evening," she replied as the taxi turned into her driveway. Hugo and Pharrell watched as Lucy safely made her way inside. They saw her son wave at the door before the taxi pulled away into the main road.

***

"Hello, Mr. Lebervitz…It's Jac," the private detective hollered down the telephone.

"Yes…Go ahead, what have you got for me?" Harry abruptly asked.

Jac realised that Harry Lebervitz had no time for small talk. "I have found out that the Louvre are interested in purchasing the pa…py…ri, is that how you say it."

"Papyri…Yes what else have you found out?"

"Hugo and Pharrell met with Lucy Bouchard and went to a jazz club and then onto a casino last night. It looked like they were celebrating something."

"Have you anything else, for me?" Harry asked.

"No."

"Try and find out what price they are asking for the papyri? And get back to me as soon as you can, is that understood?"

"Ok, Mr. Lebervitz." The phone went dead before he finished speaking. He realised Harry Lebervitz had made his money without the need for small talk, a shrewd businessman but a rude one, he thought.

Jac decided he would call a friend from the old days in the foreign legion; he was now living in America working at the French Embassy in New York the last time they spoke. He needed to know more about Harry Lebervitz before he proceeded with his plan to extract more money if he could.

***

Pharrell and Hugo had got tired of waiting for the spectrograph results. Their forays into the city were interesting for Pharrell, but he noticed that Hugo's patience was on a knife edge. He guessed that the pressure of waiting around for news from Lucy was taken its toll on Hugo. Hugo was eager to make a deal and return to Thailand as soon as possible, and he said as much many times to Pharrell, while they waited for Lucy to phone with news. As the days passed he had phoned again Angelique's office and finally spoke with her. She had expressed her apologies and told him she had tried many times to phone him. She also told him that she would be returning to Thailand within a few days and hoped that they would see each other again soon. Pharrell was pleased to speak to Angelique, but decided not to mention on the phone how he felt about her, and he also declined to mention his plans to go to Egypt. He would wait until he saw Angelique in Bangkok and see how she felt about him. Perhaps,

Angelique was a butterfly when it came to love, here one minute and gone the next, he wasn't sure.

In a bar along the road from their hotel Hugo told Pharrell about Harry's man that he believed had been following them everywhere they went.

"I did notice a few times the other night at the casino you glance around as if you were looking for someone," Pharrell remarked.

"I didn't want to alarm Lucy, but that car, the blue Citroën that we have spotted following us on several occasions. I believe its Harry Lebervitz's man. I noticed him first at the Jazz Club and then at the casino, so I'm sure he is following us. And I'm sure he's working for Harry, it's the sort of thing Harry would do. I told you before what happened in America and how I found out that I was being followed. But don't worry Pharrell. Harry is not sort of person to harm us, he just wants to cover all bases…as the Americans say."

"Perhaps, you should phone Harry and tell him what we know…I mean about the papyri and the reason for the delay?"

"No, we will wait until we hear from Lucy," Hugo replied.

"Is the papyri safe at the hotel?" Pharrell asked intently.

"No…I have moved it, since the day we first noticed the blue Citroën following us."

"Where, Hugo?"

"At the back of our hotel there is a path leading to the main road parallel to this road. On that main road is the Paribas bank. I have a safe deposit box there," Hugo explained.

"I wondered why it took you so long the other day to fetch the papyri, while I waited in the taxi," Pharrell said.

"At least, I can sleep at night knowing the papyri are safe in the bank, just in case whoever is following us decides to steal the papyri from our hotel. If its Harry's man, he would know by now the value of the papyri, and perhaps try to steal it from the hotel's safe."

***

"How long have you been an agent for the C.I.A…Fabio?" Sarah asked inquisitively as she sipped a cool beer and looked into Fabio's eyes waiting to see his reaction.

"It must be about five years now, before joining the C.I.A. I worked in military intelligence based at Fort Worth. How about you…what's your background?" Fabio asked curiously eager to keep the conversation friendly and at the same time build a relationship with his new working partner.

Sarah thought for a moment before replying, she had a quick glance around the bar and noticed several of her colleagues from work were also there enjoying a drink after finishing a day's work. Tongues would chatter tomorrow, she said to herself.

"Not long after I finished my Masters in Politics at U.C.L.A. I joined the F.B.I. recruitment program. After several years as a desk jockey…I made field agent working low level cases and then progressed up the ladder to the position and responsibility I currently hold." Sarah replied.

"What made you want to join the F.B.I….you could have had a career in politics?" Fabio asked keenly seeking to find out what made Sarah tick, he needed to understand her motives just in case the two of them found themselves in a difficult and dangerous situation. He had read her profile and the rest of the F.B.I agents working at the Washington Inquirer back at C.I.A.

headquarters before arriving at the magazine enterprise and up to now Sarah had told him nothing he already knew, but he felt she was holding back something, he thought.

Sarah realised Fabio was eagerly trying to dig deeper into her background than she wanted to go and decided to answer the question with a familiar answer she had used many times before when asked what her motives were for joining the F.B.I. after leaving university. "I like the idea of chasing criminals," she said, with a cute smile that she knew men found attractive.

"Oh…I see…Just chas…."

Before Fabio had time to finish his sentence Sarah decided to interrupt him. "I fancy a game of pool." Sarah was already walking towards the pool table before Fabio could finish his words.

Fabio realised Sarah was in no mood for further questioning about her background and decided to play along for now. Besides, he felt sure she would tell him at some point, he believed.

Sarah noticed how Fabio eyed her body motions as she played her shots on the pool table. She knew most men found her attractive and Fabio was no different, she caught sight of him glancing down her blouse each time she leaned over the pool table to take her shot. She decided, now would be a good time to find out why the C.I.A was interested in the Thailand case.

She decided to ask a question she knew Fabio would not be willing to answer just to see his reaction. "Why is the C.I.A. interested in the Thailand case?"

"Were you not listening Sarah at the briefing?" he asked smiling.

"No…Tell me again."

"The gun smuggling and the terrorist threat," Fabio said offhandedly.

"Is that the real reason?" Sarah asked knowing Fabio could not answer unless he had clearance from his superiors.

Fabio just smiled at Sarah and continued drinking his beer without answering Sarah's direct question knowing that revealing the real reason was a national security secret.

***

"Good news, Pharrell…Lucy has the spectrograph results."

"When do we see her?" Pharrell asked keenly aware that Hugo was eager to hear what Lucy had to say. Day by day, Pharrell had noticed the pressure building on Hugo. Hugo had become irritated at the slightest thing. Even Pharrell his friend and business partner had irritated Hugo as each day had passed without news of the spectrograph results. Pharrell decided not to mention anything concerning the papyri to Hugo while they waited for news; he felt it was better to keep quiet on the subject.

"Today, at the university…at midday," Hugo replied his face showed the relief that finally the wait was over. Pharrell noticed how quickly Hugo had changed. He was the friend he knew again, happy and jolly about life. Hugo's appetite soon reappeared at breakfast. He had eaten copious amounts of his favourite ham and eggs washed down with several coffees that was the real Hugo, he mused.

"What do we do in the meantime?"

"Try and lose the tail…No doubt that Harry's man is out there waiting for us to follow. Today, we need to lose the tail…So that Harry's man gets worried, and perhaps reports back to Harry that he's failed to follow us."

"How do we do that…Hugo?" Pharrell asked intently and curious what Hugo had in mind.

"Simple, *mon cher*. We call two taxis, one for each of us. When we leave, Harry's man will see us leave separately, and he will have to decide who to follow. When we are sure which of us he is following, and hopefully for the plan to work he is driving the blue Citroën we will contact each other by mobile. Most likely, he will choose to follow me, but if he doesn't the plan can work just as well. After a considerable distance from our hotel I will enter a shop and ask the taxi to wait for a short time, knowing that I will leave the shop using a back entrance where you will be waiting in the taxi. Do you understand?"

"Yes…I see your thinking," Pharrell replied.

"Good…Let's finish breakfast and get into action."

"Why don't we just go out the back of the hotel?"

"Simple, Pharrell…I don't want Harry's man to know about the path at the back of the hotel. Just in case he comes looking for the papyri," Hugo explained.

"OK…I understand."

As Hugo and Pharrell got into separate taxis and went their separate ways the blue Citroën followed Hugo's taxi as he had predicted.

"Hello, Pharrell…Meet me at the Paribas Bank on the boulevard du Montpelier. Is that understood in five minutes," Hugo instructed.

"OK…Paribas Bank on the boulevard du Montpelier in five minutes," Pharrell repeated the instructions over the mobile phone.

As Hugo got out of the taxi in front of the main post office he told the taxi to wait five minutes for him and then he generously tipped the taxi driver. He already knew the post office had two entrances one on each parallel street. He hoped Harry's man would wait seeing that the taxi had not pulled away.

As Pharrell's taxi waited in front of the Paribas Bank for Hugo, Pharrell felt the heat of the day as sweat gently rolled down his face as he sat on the back seat of the taxi in anticipation of Hugo's arrival. The last two weeks had been a revelation as Hugo's business partner, he mused. The art world was a business of fakes and forgeries, of conmen and thieves where huge sums of money traded hands and the stress and pressure was not for the faint hearted. But, he enjoyed the excitement of finding rare antiquities even though at times, he understood its dangers and was willing to take the risks and follow his quest his heart told him until otherwise. He could be married and settled down now, running his book shop in Stavanger or some other suitable place in relative peace and comfort.

Hugo was almost out of breath as he opened the taxi door and climbed into the back seat. He spoke in French to the taxi driver and they were on their way to the University of Paris to see Lucy.

"Hopefully, Harry's man will report to Harry that he failed to follow us," Hugo said.

"He will now know, we know we are being followed," Pharrell remarked candidly.

"Not necessarily, *mon cher*. I went into the post office and out the other exit. If Harry's man didn't anticipate this then he just over looked the possibility because he was watching the taxi until the taxi pulled away."

As the taxi arrived at the entrance of the university Hugo and Pharrell saw the multitude of students heading from one lecture room to another. Hugo commented to Pharrell about his time as a student when he first met Lucy at university and Pharrell agreed that he also had good memories of his time at university.

"*Merci beaucoup,*" the taxi driver said, as Hugo generously paid the taxi driver. Hugo and Pharrell continued to talk about their days at university as they made their way to Lucy's office.

"What did you study at university?" Hugo asked.

"Literature...I always had a love of books from an early age. My parents ran an antique shop in Stavanger and I would read many of the books that came through the shop in my spare time...It became an obsession. There was not much else to do during the winter in Norway but while away the time reading," Pharrell replied.

"So, I guess I should call you a bookshop guru...hey, Pharrell?" Hugo said laughing as Pharrell smiled with agreement at Hugo's compliment.

"I never saw myself as a guru, but now you mention it...Yes, you could call me a bookshop guru. I like the compliment...It fits in well with my occupation, experience and love of books. I probably need to move to somewhere like India and fulfil my destiny as a guru. I can see myself now...As a guru with a mass of followers," Pharrell replied laughing with Hugo as they neared Lucy's office.

Lucy was at her desk busy peering at a document as Pharrell and Hugo were led into Lucy's office by her assistant. "Take a seat I have some interesting news for you," she said as she peered above her spectacles with a tone of excitement in her voice.

"I have here the English translation of the Greek text from the spectrograph scanning and I think you will find it most interesting, Hugo," she said hardly able to contain her excitement. "Here...take a look for yourself."

Pharrell watched as Hugo's face turned to a bundle of joy as he read the document. "*mon ami,*" he said as his hands were shaking as he passed the document to Pharrell to read.

Pharrell began to read the document. *According to legend the Arc of the Covenant...*

"Can this be true?" Hugo asked with glee in his voice. "This will make the papyrus a hot item to sell...Everyone will want to buy it."

Lucy replied, "It's there in black and white...a spectrograph does not lie."

Pharrell asked without wishing to spoil the party and not completely sure he should be asking the questions. "Are you sure about the date and the translation?"

Lucy's eyes lids fluttered and her jaw dropped at Pharrell's suggestion that perhaps her translation or date were somehow erroneous. "No, they are correct," she said in a harsh tone peering directly at Pharrell with eyes as cold as ice.

"Sorry...I didn't mean to doubt your expertise, Lucy...it's just...well, and you know in this business the fakes and forgeries are everywhere. You just have to be careful...and I guess I over reacted, Pharrell said trying desperately to placate Lucy without sounding condescending.

"No, Pharrell's right," Hugo said with a soft tone reflecting his concern. "Are you sure, Lucy?"

"Yes, I am Hugo. The date is a lot harder to nail down. But, the text translation is verbatim using how Greek was used back in that time and the obvious English equivalent," Lucy replied with authority in her voice.

Hugo asked, "Why is the date a problem?"

Lucy replied with a hint of annoyance in her voice at the interrogation by Hugo and Pharrell. "I didn't say the date was a problem...I merely said it was a lot harder to nail down exactly. Carbon dating is not an exact science...it is being constantly improved. Carbon dating can give a date within one hundred years or so at present. The style of Greek used can also reveal an approximate time frame."

Hugo said, "The document says that the Arc of the Covenant was secretly moved by the priests from the temple during the Babylonian siege of Jerusalem."

Lucy said, "Yes, we know the date King Nebuchadnezzar laid siege to Jerusalem, which was in the year five hundred and eighty six B.C. approximately. And we know the date of the carbon dating of the papyrus, which is around five hundred eighty and three hundred eighty B.C. and we know the date of the later text found on the papyrus is around the time of the birth of Christ. So the hidden text revealed by the spectrograph suggests a date of between five hundred and eighty B.C. and the birth of Christ. Now, can you see Hugo what I mean by difficult to nail down the date?"

"Yes, I understand what you mean, Lucy," Hugo replied.

"You must remember that the scribe was writing in past tense," she added.

"Yes, we understand this. Have you an idea why the original text was washed away?"

"Most likely a Jewish scribe wanted to hide the text, but also wanted to reuse the papyrus. Don't forget the hidden text is about a legend and perhaps during the revolt by the Maccabees against the Greeks the scribe decided to wash away the text rather than burn a valuable piece of papyrus."

Pharrell interrupted wishing to move the conversation forward without upsetting Lucy's sensibilities anymore, "Perhaps a scholar will find some clues hidden within the translation. The text mentions the Arc of the

Covenant was moved out of the city before the Babylonians arrived and then it travelled by sea."

Lucy said with calmness having explained her reasoning to Pharrell and Hugo sufficient to reassert her authority again, "Yes, you are right Pharrell…a scholar would indeed find this text intriguing and value its place in history…especially the Jews. The Jews have been searching for the Arc since they founded the state of Israel." She curled her hair with both hands and added with a cute smile, "To the Jews this piece of history is almost like finding the Dead Sea Scrolls. Its value is beyond money I would assume."

Hugo's mind immediately started to think of the possibilities. He had an idea, but he needed to discuss it with Pharrell first, but not in front of Lucy, he thought. "I will need to see your man at the Louvre again," he said to Lucy with his mind running ahead at the possibilities.

"Oh, Michel Napier…Yes, I am sure the Louvre would like to acquire it," Lucy said.

"Can I have a copy of your translation and a copy of the Greek text…And of course the original papyrus back?" Hugo asked politely not expecting Lucy's rebuke.

"Of course, Hugo…was you expecting something else?" she said with a tone in her voice that implied she was upset with him about something.

Hugo just pretended to be mystified and shrugged his shoulders. Then it clicked in his mind he had not paid Lucy. "Have I not paid you for the work you did for me?" he asked play-acting to deflect the annoyance he had caused. He quickly wrote a cheque and doubled the amount they had previously agreed hoping this would in some way compensate for his absent-mindedness, he supposed.

Lucy gratefully received the cheque from Hugo and suggested he see a doctor about his amnesia. They all laughed at Lucy's joke and then they discussed meeting again for another night out together before Hugo and Pharrell made their plans to return to Thailand.
In the taxi on their way back to their hotel Hugo began explaining his idea to Pharrell. "Listen...I have idea how we can maximise the selling price of the papyruses." Pharrell observed how Hugo's complexion had changed. He could see the redness of Hugo's face and felt the excitement in Hugo's voice as he began to tell him his idea. "We could split the papyruses...sell the papyrus containing the hidden text about the Arc of Covenant to the Jews and offer the other papyri to the Louvre. What do you think, Pharrell?"
"When you say the Jews...Do you mean Harry Lebervitz?"
"Yes, perhaps...but there are numerous Jewish organisations, collectors and museums that would want to acquire anything associated with the Arc of the Covenant," Hugo said eager to convince Pharrell of his reasoning.
"This would mean waiting longer...I thought you wanted to sell as quickly as possible and return to Thailand?" Pharrell asked with thoughts in his mind about his return to Thailand. He wanted to return to Thailand, now that Angelique had phoned him. He had to persuade Hugo, he said to himself.
"Yes, I did. But, think about the opportunity to capitalise on finding that hidden text." Hugo said remonstrating with his hands at Pharrell. "This could mean a lot more money in our pockets." Pharrell noticed several times the taxi driver looking at his rear view mirror at Hugo's bodily actions and trying to understand the old man's excitement. Perhaps, the taxi

driver thinks Hugo had won the lottery, Pharrell said to himself.

"I think you need to think this out carefully, Hugo…when you divide something it's always weaker." Pharrell said calmly trying to convince Hugo to stick to the original plan.

"So, you don't think we should sell the papyruses separately?" Hugo asked eager to understand the reasons why Pharrell had misgivings on his idea.

"No, because the longer we delay the more likely something happens we didn't see coming and wish then that we had stayed with the original plan," Pharrell replied hoping Hugo would calm down and see sense.

"I understand your logic, but is that the real reason?" Hugo asked curious to find out why Pharrell was so dead against his plan.

"Look at this…this way Hugo. We can achieve a good price for the papyri together rather than split it between different buyers. And we can then move forward. I will be honest I need to get back to Thailand and also my quest. I promised to help when you said a few days in Algeria and that turned into several weeks. If you want to sell separately then that's your choice, but I need to get back to Thailand in a few days' time," Pharrell said with a commanding tone in his voice and not willing to be persuaded.

Pharrell saw that Hugo looked dejected, his face had lost its glow of excitement that his plan had not found favour. "You are perhaps right, Pharrell…I will need to think it over and of course talk with Ning," Hugo said settling into a quieter mood as the taxi neared their hotel.

Hugo caught a glance of a blue Citroën parked a short distance from their hotel as their taxi stopped in front of their hotel, he was certain it was Harry's man, he said to himself.

***

"Hello…It's Jac."

"Go ahead…What have you for me?" Harry Lebervitz asked in the usually brusque manner over the phone without the courtesy of saying hello.

"Today, I believe Hugo and Pharrell know that they are being followed. This morning, they took separate taxis from their hotel. So, I followed Hugo. He went into the Post Office on the boulevard du Montpelier. I waited outside in the car because the taxi also waited outside for around five minutes before driving away. I immediately got out of the car and walked into the Post Office looking for him. He must have used the rear exit and onto the boulevard du Artiste," Jac explained his oversight expecting Harry to be annoyed at the news. On the contrary and to his amazement, he heard just the faint sounds of murmurs and the occasional grunt over the phone as he explained what happened.

"Have you found out the price Hugo is offering for the papyri to the Louvre?" Harry asked without waiting for Jac to finish his report. "This information is important," he said with a harsh tone in his voice.

"I have Mr Lebervitz," Jac replied hoping to hear some encouraging words, but none were forthcoming. "Hugo is asking one million dollars and…," Jac replied before having a chance to finish the sentence.

"How did you find out this information…no strong arm tactics I hope? Remember, what I told you at the beginning of this assignment…I don't want anyone hurt. Do you understand?"

"Loud and clear Mr. Lebervitz, it's not how I work," Jac said knowing that he was lying. "Michel Napier keeps a diary and records of all his meetings with clients at the Louvre. I simply waited for him to go to lunch today, and entered his office and found the diary."

"Good…is there anything else to report?"

"Yes. Mr. Napier made a comment in his diary. It said the Louvre, are willing to purchase the papyri if the papyri pass their examination."

"Good news…right Mr. Lebervitz?" Jac asked.

"Anything else, you have forgotten to tell me?"

"No," Jac replied and then the phone went dead.

***

The daily briefing at the Washington Inquirer started as normal that morning with the section chief giving his daily report of progress on the operational case.

"Our agent in Miramar reports that a container ship is due to arrive with a cargo of guns from China in two days' time. The cargo's final destination is at present unknown," the section chief said, stressing in his voice the importance of the upmost secrecy when reporting intelligence to this office. "As you known the C.I.A. have assigned their agent to liaison all intelligence agencies. They have requested that all knowledge of their involvement in our operational case be restricted to those present in this room. Also, all files and reporting of gun smuggling will be referred to using the code word *Dragon.*" The section chief remonstrating with his hands drew one hand across his neck and said, "The C.I.A want to cut the head off the dragon." Staring at his colleagues around the room as he stood before them the section chief's said with the harsh voice of a General rallying his troops before a battle, "Now, go to work!"

"Sir, I leave on Tuesday for Bangkok."

"I would prefer you address me as Tom and not sir…it sounds so military Sarah."

***

"Hello is that professor Frieda Maupin," Pharrell asked holding the phone to his ear as close as possible to hear the professor above the noise created by a group of excited school children joining the queue to see the studios of the great artist Toulouse Lautrec. "Your contact details were given to me by Henri Piccar. I understand you have an interesting theory about the early development of man that I would like to hear. Can I come and see you?"

"Yes, of course. What did you say your name was?" she said in English with a French accent. Pharrell noticed the reflection in her pronunciation as she spoke each word carefully and obviously had much practice speaking English, he surmised.

"Pharrell Anderson." Pharrell raised the tone of his voice without shouting so the Professor could clearly hear his name above the background noise in the art studios. "Would around six this evening…is that okay? Can I also bring along my friend and business partner Hugo Deschamps?"

"Did you say Hugo Deschamps…a very good friend of Henri and Cherie Piccar?" she said repeating Hugo's name to Pharrell without hesitation and with excitement clearly audible in her voice.

"Yes, that's right." Pharrell was not surprised the professor knew Hugo. Hugo had spent most of his life in France before moving to Thailand he had told him previously. Although at times Hugo's influence occasionally annoyed him, his friendship with Hugo had lasted over the years. He was almost like a father figure to him, someone he could trust.

"Yes, of course. I have known Hugo for many years. Bring him along; it will be fun to catch up on old times," she said confidently expressing herself to Pharrell with only the slightest hint that English was not her native tongue. "Come to my office at the University of Paris."

Hugo explained how the artist Toulouse Lautrec would spend many hours painting everyday life. Toulouse had a passion for the show girls and this was demonstrated in many of his Parisian paintings of the bohemian night life. The French people have a special love affair with Lautrec's work because it signified a period in the history of France when the French people felt liberated, and as Hugo explained it was a period when art and fashion were in vogue, and not just for the rich but for the common man as well. The tour of Toulouse Lautrec's studio had been an interesting afternoon distraction for Hugo and Pharrell.

"How do you know Professor Maupin?" Pharrell asked Hugo as their taxi made its way to the university.

"Paris is a huge city, but has a small fraternity of intellectuals that meet yearly at conventions. Over the many years of living in Paris you get to know each other," Hugo replied. "By the way, I have arranged to for us to see Harry Lebervitz tomorrow at midday at his hotel. Hopefully we can strike a deal with him and be on our way back to Thailand in a few days."

"Have you decided to sell the papyri complete?" Pharrell asked.

"Yes, I thought it over and it makes sense to keep the papyri together. Besides, you are right it's better to sell now and enjoy our good fortune rather than wait, and then who knows what perhaps may happen."

"Follow the signs to the anthropology department," Pharrell said to the taxi driver who turned around and looked at Pharrell perplexed at these instructions in English. "Sorry, I forget not everyone understands English," he said to the taxi driver. The taxi driver waved his hand with satisfaction as Hugo repeated the instructions to him in French.

As the taxi stopped in front of the anthropology building Pharrell and Hugo thanked the taxi driver who seemed in a hurry they thought. As the taxi sped away without waiting for several students stood nearby who were clearly trying to catch his attention. Perhaps, the taxi driver was eager to get home, Pharrell mused.

The anthropology building was clearly a new building it had a modern façade compared to Lucy Bouchard's department, Pharrell thought. The building was quiet as most students had gone home for the day as Hugo and Pharrell looked around for someone they could ask for directions. They came upon a janitor cleaning the floor who was able to give Hugo directions to Professor Maupin's office. The janitor had chuckled and said something to himself as Hugo thanked the man.

Professor Maupin's office was on the top floor of the building with panoramic views of the campus. Just as they were about to remark to each other about how big the campus was they heard the sound of footsteps approaching them. "Can I help you," said the woman.

"*Oui*, we are here to see Professor Maupin," Hugo replied in French.

"Follow me," the woman said.

As they passed many doors in the corridor Hugo turned to Pharrell and said, "I forgot to ask you what anthropology has to do with your quest."

Pharrell replied, "I'm not sure, but Henri Piccar gave me a list of contacts and Professor Maupin was on that list."

Pharrell and Hugo were greeted by the professor with a hand shake. Her long dark auburn hair curled upon her shoulders and the colour of her hair matched her brown eyes. Her sleek and slender body added to the attractiveness of the middle-age woman, she had the facial looks of Spanish decent, possibly Moorish, Pharrell thought.

"Hello Hugo, long time...and you must be Pharrell Anderson. Welcome and please take a seat. Oh, please call me Frieda."

"How can I help you?" Frieda asked.

"As you know Henri Piccar gave me your contact details. Apparently, you have a theory on the evolution of man. Although, I'm not sure how this relates to my quest."

"And your quest is?" Frieda asked in a candid manner.

"Have you heard about the legend, the so called *Shahbla el Allah* or loosely translated in English, *the book of God*?" Pharrell asked expecting an affirmative answer.

"No...I can't say I have," Frieda replied in a matter of fact way.

"Never mind, please tell us your theory," Pharrell said eager to listen to the professor's theory.

"You, no doubt, have heard about Darwin's theory of evolution," Freida hesitated momentarily as she stared at Hugo and Pharrell for their facial reaction. "In Darwin's book the *Origins of Species* he puts forward a theory that he called *Natural Selection.* He also suggested that all living organisms originate from a single cell on what he called the tree of life. He viewed this tree upside down to a single stem and the branches of the tree would represent the different species. Now, over time...many millions of year's species would evolve, but with common ancestors because of the branches represented on the tree of live. Because of the way we inherit genes, and, those genes with characteristics beneficial to the organism through Darwin's theory of *Natural Selection* each progressive generation would pass on those genes to the next generation and so on. So, over a considerable amount of time a new species would evolve on a different branch of the *tree of life,* but, with a common ancestor. I have summarised pages and pages of theory into a few sentences, so I hope you are following the essence so far of Darwin's theory?" Frieda said waiting for Hugo and Pharrell to acknowledge they understood what so far she had said.

"Please, continue...Frieda," Pharrell said.

"Now, this is where it gets interesting," she said raising the tone of her voice to announce to Hugo and Pharrell they should listen carefully to what she now had to say. "Darwin decided to publish his theory after many years of research, but also after many years of deliberation, because he had major doubts about his conclusions. He was almost cajoled into publishing at the time by a friend and the publisher because another naturalist Alfred Wallace was about to publish his theory that was essentially the same as Darwin's theory of evolution."

"What was the problem?" Hugo asked intrigued to know the reasons why Darwin was unsure about his theory of *Natural Selection.*

Frieda said smiling, "You haven't changed...Hugo...your lack of patience is indeed a characteristic. Darwin was unsure because he couldn't quite square through his theory of *natural selection*...how we...that is, how humans developed intelligence. There are other issues as well that I will get to later. Can you understand the problem and the issues so far?"

"Yes, but it's not how we were taught at school," Pharrell remarked.

Hugo agreed, "Yes, but what has this to do with Pharrell's quest? It doesn't make sense. Why would Henri consider your theory important to Pharrell?

Frieda said shrugging her shoulders, "It beats me...Hugo. But, let me finish. I haven't told you my theory yet."

"Okay. Continue Frieda. Never mind me, you know I lack the patience of a Saint," Hugo replied smiling at his cute remark to Frieda.

"You are right, Pharrell. Every schoolchild is taught the same throughout the world. Darwin's theory of *Natural Selection* has never been seriously challenged because the main stream establishment of science considers it to be a sound theory. And, every time a scientist puts forward a flaw in Darwin's theory the establishment come up with a plausible reason to argue against this," Frieda said eagerly watching their reactions as she laid the groundwork before revealing her theory.

"Before I layout my theory it's important to understand the meaning of anthropology. The term anthropology originates from the Greek *anthrōpos* meaning humankind; therefore, as an anthropologist my role is the study of humans past and present using the collective knowledge of archaeological, biological, cultural, linguistic, and social disciplines." Frieda paused and looked at Pharrell and Hugo for several seconds to gauge their reactions before then continuing. "As you know *Homo Sapiens* is the scientific classification for the human race or species and the only surviving species of the homo genus of which there were several human species coexisting until relatively recent times such as the Neanderthals."

Frieda paused briefly to catch her breath and to curl some of her auburn hair into place behind her ears. She caught sight of Hugo watching her every move. She wondered if Hugo had any feelings for her. She knew from the past how Hugo would flirt with the ladies at conventions and parties, but perhaps being older he had slowed down, she mused.

"Recent DNA studies have found that most Europeans have between one percent and four percent of their genes inherited from the Neanderthals, so contrary to previous scientific understanding there was interbreeding between the two human species. The scientific establishment have only recently acknowledged this fact, before it was unthinkable for science to believe the possibility of such a suggestion." Frieda said emphasizing her words with a tonal change in her voice.

"I didn't know that…but it makes sense…physically the same species living together in the same environment are at some point are going to interbreed…its nature," said Pharrell.

"I agree…you cannot argue against the proof of DNA evidence," Hugo agreed.

"I'm glad you said physically the same species, Pharrell…because for similar species to interbreed they have to be of the same kind…in this case Homo which really means humankind," Frieda said.

"I still don't know what all this has to do with my quest, but, please continue."

"There is much conjecture within the science community why there is a missing link in our evolutionary history as a species. Some argue that it's because archaeologists just haven't found the evidence yet. Their proposition is that bones decay relatively easy in acidic soils, so the evidence is difficult to find and that is why so few bone samples of early man survive. The science community is divided on what was our common ancestor; this is often referred to as the missing link in our evolutionary history."

Pharrell and Hugo listened intently as the professor was clearly enjoying her lecture. Only pausing occasionally, Frieda had a gift in how she told a story.

"But, keep in mind there are also many missing links in the animal kingdom such as the missing link between fish and amphibians, you would have expected many different stages of development with a fossil record at each stage, but none have been found. Even Darwin was puzzled by this lack of fossil record, even though his theory of gradual changes of a species champions over a considerable amount of time, many millions of years that through *natural selection* ultimately you derive a series of new species with a distant common ancestor. Now, you would expect to see the distinct changes in the fossil record, but we don't have those missing links."

"Perhaps, they haven't been found, yet," Hugo remarked and then realising he should have kept quiet.

"If you believe in Darwin's theory then all life on this earth started with a single cell and then multicellular organisms evolved and these branched off into separate branches forming new organisms and so on, as explained in Darwin's tree of life. So, some of our genes in the Human Genome should not be unique as they would have to be inherited at each stage of our evolutionary development on the tree of life. So, why do we have a gene that is present in no other organism except humans called *Fox −P2?* Where did this gene come from, it exists in no other organism?

Pharrell keenly asked, "What is your theory, Frieda?"

"Although there have been published attempts through artificial insemination to crossbreed and produce a hybrid between our closest evolutionary relative the chimpanzee that has around ninety four percent identical DNA to humans the results so far have been unsuccessful." Frieda said, before pausing to see the reaction from her audience.

"Yes, what is your theory, Frieda," Hugo asked, hoping for a *coup d'etat* or an end to the lecture.

"Okay, it's not my own theory, although, myself and many other leading scientists and anthropologists support the theory. The theory is called the *Special Event Theory*. The theory's proposition is that our intelligence and language abilities cannot be a product of evolution as described in Darwin's theory of *Natural Selection* because according to current archaeological discoveries they appeared to evolve in a relatively short space of time in evolutionary terms, and not the millions of years suggested by Darwin's theory of *Natural Selection*. Current archaeological discoveries suggest that man developed the ability to use sophisticated tools, and the ability to record their thoughts on cave walls, and one would assume the ability of language around 40,000 to 50,000 years ago. And, so what was so special then that all three abilities evolved at around the same time? Leading scientists and anthropologists argue that a special event must have taken place.

Frieda continued explaining the *Special Event Theory* with a series of examples to further her argument on the plausibility of the theory. She could see from their facial expressions that Hugo and Pharrell were not totally convinced.

"An interesting theory, Frieda, but, what has this theory got to do with the *Shahbla el Allah* and my quest to find it? Pharrell asked with a look of bewilderment on his face.

"I'm not sure; perhaps, Henri and Cherie Piccar wanted you hear my theory because there's some sort of relationship between the two."

Hugo interrupted, "If I know Henri there's a hidden message. Instead of telling you direct, Pharrell, perhaps now that you have this information you are more likely to be open-minded during your quest."

"I believe I understand what you're saying, Hugo. It's like the old adage – you can't see the wood for the trees or something similar. Henri is trying to tell you something, but before he can you need to be open-minded to the possibilities," Frieda said smiling at Pharrell before continuing. "What the possibilities are, I'm not sure?"

Hugo and Pharrell thanked Frieda for her time, and on the way back to their hotel continued the discussion on the merits or not of the *Special Event Theory*. Hugo kept a look out for the blue Citroën, but it was nowhere to be seen. Perhaps, Harry's man had a day off, he said to himself.

***

The following day Hugo and Pharrell were on their way to Harry Lebervitz's hotel. The Hilton hotel was busy with people gathering in the main reception area as Pharrell and Hugo entered through the revolving doorway. There must be a convention at the hotel of some sort, Pharrell thought.

As they entered Harry's hotel room they saw Harry's wife eagerly awaiting their arrival, she had prepared a tray of hot drinks. They could smell the unmistakeable aroma of coffee percolating the room as they were ushered to sit down.

"You know my wife, whom I trust when it comes to business," Harry said after sipping a mouthful of hot coffee.

Pharrell and Hugo both nodded their heads with agreement as they sampled the coffee. "You make a nice coffee, Mrs Lebervitz," Hugo remarked smiling at Harry's wife before fixing his attention to Harry. Hugo handed the results of the carbon dating and the spectrograph of the papyri to Harry before continuing drinking his coffee.

Harry read the documents and then handed them to his wife to read. "What does this mean?"

"It means the value of papyruses has increased because of the spectrograph revealing hidden text relating to the legend of the *Arc of the Covenant*." Hugo replied in a matter of fact way without revealing any weakness in negotiations from his body language or voice.

"What price are you asking now?" Harry asked with a scowl on his face and a harshness in his voice directed at Pharrell and Hugo.

"The original asking price without any discounts one million dollars," Hugo replied without the slightest hint in the tone of his voice that he was not embarrassed in asking so much more than before. He decided to stay silent and wait for Harry's reaction before continuing negotiations, it was always a good ploy, he said to himself.

"Why are you now asking for more money?" Harry's wife asked with the same angry tone in her voice as her husband had.

"I'm sorry to upset you Mrs Lebervitz, but the papyruses are worth considerable more because as you can appreciate the spectrograph results revealing text about the legend of the Arc of the Covenant," Hugo replied focusing his attention at Mrs Lebervitz. "There will be considerable interest from Jewish collectors, Jewish organisations, and museums around the world because of this.

Pharrell said, "We are here today to offer you the chance to purchase first. Hugo and I thought you would see the potential of acquiring a piece of Jewish history.

Hugo agreed, "We both wanted to give you the chance first, but I have to add that we also have other buyers interested in purchasing the papyruses if you are not interested.

There were several minutes of silence before Harry spoke. "When do you need a decision?"

Hugo replied, "Now!" He was sure Harry knew about the Louvre and perhaps losing his tail the other day would have possibly sown some doubt in Harry's mind as to who also I have seen, he thought.

"It's...a lot of money to make a decision on the spot, besides, I would like to bargain...*kosher*," Harry said remonstrating with his hands. Perhaps, he could get the price down, he whispered to himself.

"I'm fair and honest...and we decided to offer the papyruses to you first." Hugo said repeating their offer to Harry. "You and I have done business together before, and, we both know the value of pieces of history. We need a firm decision now, because we have other buyers waiting if you decide not to purchase.

Harry looked at his wife for approval. Harry's wife asked, "What guarantee have we that it's not a fake or forgery?

Hugo calmly replied, "You have the carbon dating and spectrograph results plus the expert opinion of Lucy Bouchard a professor of antiquities at the University of

Paris and the opinion of Michel Napier at the Louvre who is an expert in papyri."

"Okay, *Kosher*," Harry said satisfied that he also knew what the Louvre were proposing to do and at the same price or more. He felt confident and assured he could make a considerable profit by selling the papyruses to the Guggenheim Museum in New York, he believed.

"When do we make the transfer?" Harry asked eager to make the deal before someone else decided to pay more than Hugo and Pharrell were asking.

"These are my bank details…as soon as I receive confirmation of the one million dollars has been transferred into my bank account then Pharrell and I will bring the papyri to you. I expect the funds within twenty four hours…is that okay? Hugo asked.

"No problem…Hugo. When I make a deal…I make a deal…*kosher*," Harry said offering his hand to Hugo to shake and then to Pharrell. Harry's wife then shook their hands before offering them more fresh coffee.

On their way back to their hotel Hugo and Pharrell again noticed from the rear window of the taxi the same blue Citroën that had been following them over several days. "Harry's man no doubt," Hugo remarked to Pharrell in a confident mood with a smile on his face.

"At least, we can get back to Thailand within a few days," Pharrell said. He was happy that he would soon see Angelique. "The negotiations went well with Harry, I thought."

"Yes, better than I expected. The ruse the other day to lose Harry's man worked well. I guess Harry's man would have told Harry, and Harry would have then wondered what we got up to. I'm sure he knew about our visit to the Louvre and perhaps more," Hugo said in a confident manner while their taxi sped its way through the streets of Paris.

"What do you mean…perhaps more?" Pharrell curiously asked.

"Well, Harry's man must be some sort of private detective. And Harry would have asked him to find out as much as possible about our visit to see Michel Napier at the Louvre. As soon as Harry knew he had competition his greed would have took over. This helped our negotiations to sell…without all this mystery then who knows whether he would have been so keen to purchase the papyri."

"But, also the hidden text…the legend of the *Arc of the Covenant* that helped," Pharrell retorted.

"Yes, that helped us achieve a higher price, but the mystery and the people we visited really convinced Harry. Don't forget he is a Jew and they like a bargain, especially, when they think they know something we don't know," Hugo said smiling.

***

"Hello, Mr. Lebervitz…its Jac."

"Ok…what do you have for me?" Harry asked in his usual brief and business like telephone manner.

Jac sensed a happier tone in Harry's voice. Perhaps, his meeting with Hugo and Pharrell at the Hilton hotel had a successful outcome, he mused. He had observed Hugo and Pharrell enter the Hilton and make their way to Harry's hotel room.

"Yesterday Hugo and Pharrell visited the University of Paris and had a meeting with Professor Frieda Maupin in the anthropology department. Their meeting lasted a considerable time almost two hours."

"Do you know what they discussed?" Harry snapped.

"No…only that the Professor is considered to be a maverick…and that she also supports a theory about the

evolution of man considered by mainstream science to be…how you say in English…bonkers." Jac replied.
"What is the professor's theory?"
This piece of information had caught Harry's attention; he felt he could sense Harry's curiosity on the phone as if he was there in Harry's hotel room with him, Jac surmised. "She proposes that human intelligence cannot be a product of evolution…she calls it the *special event* theory. Her theory is not hers alone it was first proposed by another scientist. I should add that this information is readily available on the internet…and it took me several hours to read late last night."
"Ok…what else have you found out?" Harry muttered.
"They know they are being followed…,"
"Yes, you told me that the other day," Harry said interrupting Jac as he was about to reveal more.
"No…I was about to say someone else. I traced the car details and the car is registered to the *Gendarme.*"
"How do you know this?"
"I watched the same car on several occasions follow them."
"Do you have any idea why?"
"No!" Jac could sense in Harry's voice a tone of vulnerability, and there was fear, he could sense it, he said to himself.
"Is that it?" Harry asked, abruptly.
"Yes…but, I need some more money for expenses?" Jac went on.
"Okay, fine…come to the hotel at nine tomorrow morning," Harry replied.
"Okay…Mr. Lebervitz," Jac replied as the phone line went dead.

***

As Pharrell and Hugo got into their taxi outside their hotel there was no sight of the blue Citroën. Hugo had another glance through the rear window of the taxi as the taxi pulled away from their hotel. "Harry's man has disappeared," Hugo said confidently to Pharrell as the taxi turned into the main boulevard south towards the city centre.

"Perhaps Harry Lebervitz no longer needs to have us followed?" Pharrell retorted.

"Yes…you are right, Pharrell. Harry will have what he wants or will have shortly when we deliver the papyri to him. The money was transferred into my bank account as he promised and now we will complete our end of the deal. I'm glad to see the papyri sold and later today I can arrange tickets back to Thailand," Hugo responded.

"You not planning to see Lucy then…before we leave for Thailand," Pharrell asked.

"No…did you want to?"

"Not really, but I thought you promised Lucy the other day you would have a night out together?"

"I don't want to spend another night at the casino…it will only encourage her to gamble."

"Is that the real reason, Hugo?"

"Yes and no. I thought we could say goodbye at her place. Besides, we are only friends now. It was a long time ago we were lovers," Hugo said.

As their taxi stopped in front of the Hilton Hotel the entrance was unusually busy, Pharrell thought. The taxi driver said something to Hugo in French as he paid the fare. Hugo had another glance back to see if anyone was following them as they walked through the crowd of excited teenagers. "Apparently, the news of the latest pop idol staying at the Hilton had gone viral on the internet within minutes, the taxi driver told me," Hugo explained to a bemused Pharrell as they entered the relative calm of the hotel's reception area.

"Can you inform Mr. Lebervitz in room three hundred and sixty eight that Hugo Deschamps and Pharrell Anderson are here," Hugo said to the receptionist.

"*Oui monsieur* …," the receptionist said as she dialled the room number. "Hello, Mr. Lebervitz a Mr. Deschamps and Mr. Anderson are here to see you."

"Okay, understood," the receptionist said into the phone. Turning her gaze at Pharrell and Hugo, she then said, "Mr. Lebervitz says to wait here…he will come down and meet you."

Pharrell and Hugo decided to wait in the comfort of a nearby couch with a view of the melee outside the hotel's front entrance. It was several minutes before Harry and his wife arrived and they immediately took possession of the leather folder containing the papyruses. After a cursory glance at the papyruses Harry deposited the papyruses in the hotel's safe.

Pharrell noticed Harry's demeanour had utterly changed since their last meeting. The prospect of earning a considerable sum of money, no doubt, he said to himself. But, that was the nature of the business, high risk and high returns. A chain of middle men made money but probably not the original owner, he mused.

"Let's toast until the next time," Hugo said as he raised his glass.

"Yes…let me know first…the next time you find something of interest," Harry said in a relaxed manner raising his glass with the knowledge the papyruses were locked away in the hotel's safe box.

"Pharrell…have you found out any more information helpful to your quest?" Harry's wife asked politely. Pharrell decided to give her an honest answer, but he was well aware she was probing for information.

"Yes…did you know the ancient Sumerians were the first known civilization to invent a written language?" Without waiting for a reply he asked her for information, he felt she knew because of her interest in his quest. "Tell me what you know about the *Shahbla el Allah*?" he asked curiously watching her body language for any sign that she perhaps knew more.

"I believe the same as you…a legend and perhaps a lost piece of history," she replied.

Pharrell realised she knew more than she was prepared to say. Her body language revealed as much and her answer was almost word for word the same as she had replied before. His intuition was right; she knew something important, that much he was sure of, he said to himself.

"If you find it…I would like to buy it," Harry interjected.

"Me too," Hugo said adding his appreciation to the prospect of finding the *Shahbla el Allah*.

"I'm sure there will be many buyers if I find it," Pharrell said knowing he would offer the chance to Hugo before Harry Lebervitz and his wife.

"Mrs Lebervitz," Pharrell said calmly waiting for her attention so he could proceed with his question. "Why are you so interested in the *Shahbla el Allah*?" Pharrell asked observing her body language. Pharrell saw how the direct question caused her to adjust her sitting position in the luxurious leather armchair allowing her time to think of a reply. For a moment Mrs. Lebervitz looked uncomfortable, he thought.

"Like you I've had an interest in finding the *Shahbla el Allah* since the first time I heard about it at university. At university, I studied art majoring in religious art. When I was told, in a lecture one day about the legend of the *Shahbla el Allah*, and from that day I've been hooked like a junkie…you could say," she said clutching her dry Martini with both hands like holding a prize possession unwilling to let go.

"What did you learn?" Pharrell asked eager to extract any grain of information that perhaps would help his quest.

"More or less what you already know from what you have already told me? I did some further research after the lecture and over the years since. In fact, that is how Harry and I first met. I was in the New York main library doing some research one day when Harry came in and sat opposite and the rest is history…as they say," she said smiling at Harry, who looked embarrassed as his face began to blush at his personal life being discussed, Pharrell noticed.

"It's strange how chance meetings decide the destiny of many people," Hugo said eager to explain his thoughts. "I met my latest girlfriend…Ning…by chance. I needed some information on Bangkok and found a tourist bureau…where Ning worked at the time…and as you say…the rest is history."

"Some philosophers say that chance is the logic of God," Pharrell said in a matter of fact way. "They say that although the universe looks and behaves in a chaotic manner it has been proved that the universe shows signs of a deterministic pattern. This perhaps proves that although we have choices ultimately our destiny is already written in the stars…so to speak."

"An interesting idea, Pharrell…and I believe that there's a lot more we don't know then we do know. Like who's buying the next round of drinks?" Harry said laughing at his own wit and at the same time signalling it was time for another round of drinks.

Pharrell caught the eye of the waiter and ordered another round of drinks and hoped the alcohol would soon loosen Mrs. Lebervitz tongue.

"*Voulez-vous quelque chose*," the waiter asked.

Pharrell could hear the waiter say something in French to another waiter standing at the bar. "…English or American la tourists," the waiter said to his friend. "Americans give tips," the friend replied with gusto.

"Have you heard the Pilgrim's Tale?" Pharrell asked Mr. and Mrs. Lebervitz and Hugo with a tone of voice that showed he was keen to tell his story. "No…," everyone said with excitement in their voices to hear the story that Pharrell was eager to tell them.

"The story goes that a pilgrim wanted to see the Dalai Lama and ask a question. The pilgrim had to wait five years before seeing the Dalai Lama."

"What was the question?" Hugo asked impatiently.

"Hugo, you have less patience than a dog waiting to be fed," Pharrell muttered.

"The pilgrim wanted to know what the meaning of life was." Pharrell continued aware of Hugo's impatience.

"The Dalai Lama answered the pilgrim's question by asking the pilgrim why you want to know the meaning of life. The pilgrim replied, because I want to know my purpose in life?" Pharrell momentarily paused; he could see by the look in their eyes that he had captured their attention. Pharrell continued, "The Dalai Lama said, Man thinks, he is above the animal, and that he has purpose, because that is the way he is taught from birth to think, but forgets he is an animal."

Harry's wife said, "Very good…I like the story." As Harry and Hugo nodded their heads with agreement their minds momentarily thought about what had just been said.

"Would you like to hear another story?" Pharrell asked eager to keep everyone drinking and perhaps Mrs. Lebervitz would reveal something about the *Shahbla el Allah*, he mused.

"Do you like telling stories?" Mr. Lebervitz asked with a jovial tone, and was eagerly awaiting the next story from Pharrell as he drank his cognac.

"I call him the bookshop guru," Hugo said laughing at his own remark.

Pharrell said, "Yes…the bookshop guru…I think the name suits me. As a boy growing up in Stavanger, Norway where there wasn't much to do in the winter…except read books. I used to read most of the books that came through my parent's antique shop. So, I have a love of books and stories."

"Tell us the story?" Mrs Lebervitz asked.

"Okay…The story starts at the C.I.A. (Central Intelligence Agency) at Langley, Virginia, in America. There is a certain policy and process at the C.I.A. of how they select their agents. Unfortunately, this is what happened on one particular day. It's been a secret for some time for the uninitiated. But, here goes:" Pharrell said pausing momentarily to catch his breath before continuing."

"The process usually comes down to three possible agents, normally two males and one female. Don't ask me why it's like this I didn't invent the process?" Pharrell said staring into the eyes of his captive audience.

"Anyhow, the three agents were told separately what will happen next. Each possible agent was told to go into a room where they will find an envelope with their instructions to follow," Pharrell said aware that his audience of three were now fully listening as each of them slightly moved forward in their chairs so they could hear the story above the background noise of the hotel's busy bar.

"Now, as the first male goes into the room where there is only a desk with an envelope and a gun, he opens the envelope and reads the instructions. *You have only one bullet in the gun.* He is then told to go into the next room and shoot his wife there waiting for him." Pharrell paused momentarily. "Unbeknown to the agents the bullets are blanks. As the agent enters the next room he sees his wife sitting there but he cannot shoot her even though he has been trained to follow orders. He fails the test."

Pharrell pausing looked at his audience and then said, "The next male follows suit and again is given the same instructions, but he also cannot shoot his wife even after much deliberation. He also fails the test."

Pausing momentarily to take a sip of his glass of Jack Daniels, Pharrell then said, "Finally, the female goes into the first room and sees the envelope and the gun and is told to shoot her husband in the next room. After a few moments the sound of a gunshot is heard and then several loud banging noises. The examiners outside the room rush into the room, where they see the husband lying dead on the floor, the female retorts, "The bullet didn't kill him so I killed him with the chair." Pausing, Pharrell then said, "She got the job."

They all laughed with Pharrell, who then said, "Veni...Vidi...Vici...I came, I saw, I conquered."

"Very good...I love your stories...you should be a writer," Mrs. Lebervitz said. Pharrell noticed her face was rosy, the alcohol no doubt, he said to himself.

"Let's play a game...each of us tell a story...Pharrell you are excluded, just the three of us," Mrs Lebervitz said pointing with a finger.

As the waiter arrived with a fresh round of drinks Pharrell observed Mrs. Lebervitz was already eager to taste her drink as he saw how immediately she had grasped the drink from the waiter. "*Voulez-vous quelque chose*," the waiter said. There was a general agreement from everyone for another round of drinks. This was the opportunity to find out what Mrs. Lebervitz knew as the alcohol would hopefully loosen her tongue, she was holding back something, Pharrell whispered to himself.

***

As Jac entered Harry's room at the hotel he could smell the perfume of a woman present. Channel No. 5, he believed.

"Let me introduce my wife, this is Jac the private detective. After the essential introductions Harry was abrupt as usual, Jac thought.

"What have you to report?" Harry asked as though he was in a hurry to be somewhere else.

"Most of yesterday I followed them to the Hilton, they were with you for about an hour and then they went straight back to their hotel." Jac paused for a moment before continuing allowing Harry time to interrupt him, which was is usual manner. Perhaps, it was because of his wife's presence he felt he had to be courteous, he mused. "In the evening Pharrell and Hugo took a stroll down their hotel's boulevard and then they had several drinks in a local bar before returning to their hotel for the evening."

"Have you anything else to report?" Harry asked impatiently.

"Yes, I have found out what department the *Gendarme* are from. They are being followed by the art and antiquities departmental officers. At the moment, I have not been able to find out why Pharrell and Hugo are under surveillance. But, within a day or so, I should have that information for you," Jac said, now, surprised at Harry's complexion, his half-hearted smile had gone and in its place the appearance of a man who'd just seen a ghost, he thought.

"Okay…get the information as soon as you can," Harry said with a worried tone in his voice. "It's vital…in fact you can cease following Hugo and Pharrell and devout you energies into finding why the police have them under surveillance. I need to know as much as possible…*pronto,"* Harry said clearing his dry throat from the after effects of too many drinks earlier in the day celebrating with his wife the purchase of the papyruses with Pharrell and Hugo in the Hotel's main bar downstairs.

"Have you bought the papyruses?" Jac asked.

Harry looked Jac in the eyes, and said, "Who's the boss hear, I ask the questions. Your job is to provide answers…and quick.

Jac felt he had to be persistent, and repeated the question. "Have you bought the papyruses?" They both looked at each other for several seconds, like they were eyeing each up for a fight. Jac would be the Golaith and Harry the David an unequal match, he mused.

"I need to know, yes or no?" Jac asked.

"Yes, I have today," Harry replied eager to stress his annoyance at Jac's direct questioning in front of his wife. Jac realised, the tone of Harry's voice had turned harsh and business like compared to moments ago.

"Here is some more money for expenses…I was planning to discontinue with your services, but, now, I need your services until further notice. In the meantime here is a bonus for your work…you will get another bonus when you finish."

"As soon as you find out what the police are doing…don't hesitate to phone," Harry said as he shook hands with Jac, and then ushered him to the door.
"Now he's gone…what are you worried about, Harry," Harry's wife asked with her own concerns visible on her face. Her middle-age wrinkles appearing beneath the heavy make-up on her face.
"Why are the police following Hugo and Pharrell? Have I been hoodwinked? Have I been sold a fucking *fugazi* …by these *shysters?* Harry replied with a mix of Jewish slang and Italian colloquial language he often heard growing up in the Bronx, New York.
"It may be nothing…don't worry, Harry," she said half-heartedly and without conviction in her voice. "Perhaps, it's a mistake…I didn't get the feeling from Hugo or Pharrell that they were forgers. Everything seemed normal…to me. So, let's try and remain calm."
Harry looked at his wife and listened to her half-hearted attempt at placating him. He then said, "The deal looked all *kosher*…I took the right steps from the beginning. I hired a detective. I had them followed…I found out who my competitors were. I have the results from the carbon dating and the spectrograph…and they are all *kosher*.
"Maybe you are worrying for nothing…perhaps, everything is okay. Perhaps, the police surveillance is for a different matter," she said as she watched her husband pacing up and down the room, oblivious to her last sentence. "Listen," she said in a raised tone of voice, observing a reaction from her husband as he stopped and stared at her. "Let's wait for Jac…before we get angry."
"You are right, my love…but I have just invested one million in a possible *fugazi.* It's hard not to worry," Harry croaked.

"You have just said the word…possible…all we know is the French police have them under surveillance…the rest is all speculation." She said with conviction and with the knowledge that her husband was now listening to her every word.

"The loss I can live with…I think. But…the thought of being hoodwinked…now, I think I could deal with that. It's part of this business…the art market is riddled with fakes like Swiss cheese. But, reputations…imagine, what the museums and art collectors would think of me?"

"Most likely the same as before, it happens to the best in the business. Like you said the market is riddled with fakes, anyone can get caught out…but the important thing to remember is you purchased it in good faith." she said calmly to her husband who was beginning to listen, and he had finally stopped pacing the room.

"I was planning our return to New York in a few days' time, but, now, it will have to wait until we know more from Jac. Besides, I'm waiting for the export license to arrive. Just as well, I didn't try to leave the country without an export license," Harry said to his wife with a hint of melancholy in his voice clearly visible from his body posture as he sat in the chair with his hands holding his head as if in shame.

"I know you…you wouldn't even try it. Would you?" she asked in a sheepish manner.

"Of course, not, I do everything by the book. I married you…didn't I?" They both laughed and Harry was reminiscent of what his grandfather would say. "I remember what my grandfather taught me. He always used to say: *Always do the right things because it takes less energy.* If you live by this you do not have to keep looking over your shoulder and wondering who may be watching you. The more energy you consume doing the wrong things the less energy you will have to do the right things." Harry paused to catch his breath and then continued, "My grandfather would then say: *It's simple logic, but it works and safe to say you will live life with nature and not against it.*"

***

The taxi waited outside the hotel several minutes before Pharrell and Hugo were ready to leave. As Hugo got into the taxi he had a quick glance to see if the blue Citroën was anywhere to be seen, Pharrell unconsciously did the same. Hugo apologized to the taxi driver before given him instructions to Lucy Bouchard's address.
"I didn't see the blue Citroën, did you?" Hugo asked.
"No…probably Harry's man got tired and went home." Pharrell replied.
"Yes…perhaps…but, I think, now, that Harry has bought the papyruses he doesn't need a private detective following us," Hugo went on.
"Yes…you are probably right…Hugo. Anyway, let's relax and enjoy the evening with Lucy before we leave for Thailand tomorrow."
As the taxi pulled into Lucy's driveway Pharrell and Hugo caught sight of Lucy standing by the front door awaiting their arrival. "She must be psychic," Pharrell muttered.
"No, it's the gravel driveway; it makes a great deal of noise as a car approaches the house. I guess she heard the taxi from her front room," Hugo explained.
After the customary hugs and kisses Lucy ushered them into her front room. Pharrell could smell the aroma of hot coffee and the scent of fresh cut flowers in the room. Hugo gestured with his hands and looked at Pharrell to get his attention away from Lucy as he

pointed to a table with a tray of neatly cut sandwich triangles.
Lucy said, "Help yourself, just some egg and ham sandwiches."
As Hugo and Pharrell gorged on Lucy's food they heard the sound of the gravel outside grating under the wheels of a car as it approached the front door. "That'll be Thierry," Lucy said with a huge smile.
As Lucy introduced her son again to Pharrell and Hugo, Pharrell thoughts were of family life. The missing part of his life, he said to himself.
"You go back to Thailand, tomorrow?" Lucy asked with a hint of sadness in her voice.
"Yes, but only for a few days, and then I'm off to Egypt to continue my quest," Pharrell replied with the excitement of a young boy receiving a long awaited present. "And then at some point, I need to return to Norway."
"Why, Norway?" Lucy asked.
"I have an antiquarian bookshop in Stavanger, my hometown…I also sell rare books on the internet. I have Joachim, he is my best friend from childhood…he's looking after the bookshop while I'm away. He deals with everything…Joachim. We both went to the same schools. He manages the bookshop, while I go searching for rare books. He's a Godsend."
"I call him the bookshop guru," Hugo said announcing cheerfully the phrase he had coined for his friend.
Pharrell smiled at Hugo before continuing his discussion with Lucy. "I normally spend around two months every year travelling the world searching for rare books and documents." Pharrell paused; briefly to catch his breath, his thoughts were about what Frieda Maupin had said. "Do you know Professor Frieda Maupin?"

"Yes…why do you ask?" Lucy asked.

"She has a strange theory about the evolution of Man…it's not a mainstream establishment view."

"What is her theory…I'm intrigued to know more?"

Pharrell stated, "I should also say, it's not her own theory…many influential scientists believe the same…it's just not the view of the establishment. They call it the *Special Event Theory*."

"Current ideas and theories are not always the correct ones…history teaches us that," Thierry said interrupting while Pharrell paused again for breath before continuing.

"You are right Thierry…history is constantly changing…our view of the past is constantly being revised as we find new discoveries that don't quite fit what we previously believed. Essentially, the *Special Event Theory* argues that our intelligence and language abilities cannot be a product of evolution…They argue that if that is the case then why do dolphins and whales not have the same abilities as man. They say that dolphins and whales have comparatively the same size of brain for their body mass compared to man…so why have the intelligence and language abilities of dolphins and whales not evolved during the same amount of time…in evolutionary terms. That's the essence of the theory…I hope I've done it justice…because it's a lot more complicated than how I've just explained it."

Thierry interjected, "But, how can we be sure that dolphins and whales haven't developed…I mean how do we known for sure, how smart they are? Do you understand what I am trying to say, Pharrell? I don't mean to interrupt you."

Everyone looked at Pharrell waiting for him to continue. "Oh, yes, I forgot the how part…which is the most revealing and somewhat unbelievable." Pharrell then paused for a moment waiting to see if everyone was listening. "They believe several special events must have taken place in a relatively short space of time. First: The ability to communicate. Second: The ability to think abstractly. Third: The ability to record their thoughts."

Lucy interrupted perplexed at what Pharrell had said, and asked, "But, isn't that Darwin's theory that natural selection provides adaptation to environmental conditions that are beneficial and so over time a species evolves into a new species?"

"Yes…you have hit the point…time. Darwin's theory suggested a long period of time…in the millions of years…and not the relatively short space of time that current archaeological discoveries suggest," Pharrell retorted.

"What do you mean…current archaeological discoveries suggest?" Lucy asked with a bemused look on her face.

"Current archaeological discoveries suggest that man started recording their thoughts on the walls of caves around 40,000 to 50,000 years ago…it also suggests man developed sophisticated tools around this time, and you could assume that language or the ability to communicate also around this time. Now, you have to ask, why then? What was so special then…that all three abilities evolved at around the same time?" Pharrell watched their reaction to what he had just said. He had started to ask the same questions, did they think the same? He asked himself.

Thierry was first to speak, and ask Pharrell, "Do you believe in the *Special Event Theory*, Mr. Anderson?"

"You have to ask the question…was Darwin right? Now, we are all taught at school Darwin's theory of evolution, but several things just don't add up. The

Special Event Theory is plausible just as Darwin's theory has been the excepted theory for the past one hundred years or so. It's like the theory of physics you need another theory to explain the behaviour of particles of atoms' because the two don't match…if you know what I mean?

"Don't get into mathematics, you'll make it too complicated…," Hugo said trying to make everyone laugh.

"Anyway, all this information is available on the internet. I read most of what the Professor Maupin and others have published on the *Special Event Theory* after visiting her there on the campus at the University of Paris. She has an office on the other side of the campus in a new building by the statue of Renee Pascal.

"Yes, I know…the anthropology building," Thierry said eager to agree. "The building was designed by the famous Swiss architect Luigi Snozzi. Do you believe in the theory, Mr. Anderson?"

"That's the second time you have asked me, and I'm not sure if I can give you a straight yes or no, because the theory doesn't provide enough evidence to give you an answer," Pharrell replied in a matter of fact way. He was eager to continue his explanation. "It's similar for Darwin's theory; every time someone comes up with a problem they resolve it by providing a convenient solution. For example, there are those in the scientific community who say that the *Special Event Theory* is nothing more than what they call *progressive inheritance* where natural selection has speeded up to allow for new environmental factors."

"What do you believe, Mr Anderson?" Thierry asked in a final attempt to hear what Pharrell believed.

"I don't know what to believe, and that's being honest. Having read what these other scientists are proposing, you begin to doubt what you previously thought was the truth. After all, this is what is taught to school children all around the world. There seems to be more holes in Darwin's theory than holes on a golf course. They said the Coelacanth fish had been extinct for 350 million years, yet, it turns out the fish species is very much alive, and favoured by fisherman of the east coast of Africa. You have to ask yourself why this fish has not evolved in 350 million years of evolution. Darwin's theory needs serious work, and perhaps the biggest mistake in history." Pharrell said with the confidence in his voice that he had misgivings about Darwin's theory. Thierry said, "Thanks for the explanation, I now have an informed view. You should have been a teacher you have a skill in explaining clearly the facts. And, I'm leaning with you, something isn't quite right. We have been fooled, perhaps, by a theory that has become the established scientific view, yet, there are more holes in it than a straining colander." They all laughed at the same time.

With a glass of wine in one hand Hugo raised his arm and offered a toast to the successful conclusion of a deal. Hugo prompted everyone to join his toast. "Come on, everyone, raise your glass, and let's toast our good fortune!"

"Hugo is right. We have been fortunate to have made a good deal. And now it's time to thank lady luck and the Gods or God," Pharrell said with a jovial tone of voice, he was thankful the deal went ahead without any complications.

"What does this *Special Event Theory* have to do with your quest, Pharrell?" Lucy asked.

Pharrell replied, "I don't know, but the Professor Frieda Maupin was on a list of names to contact given to me by Henri and Cherie Piccar…your friends? I was going to ask you about Sheik Abdul Adin…the man you said to contact in Egypt," he said facing Lucy and waiting for her reply with anticipation.

"Not much, only what I have previously told you. The sheik has a notorious reputation…he has been caught in the past for smuggling Egyptian artefacts on several occasions," Lucy paused and said in a matter of fact manner. "What makes him interesting…he's the man to know…because not one worthwhile Egyptian artefact fails to pass his nose? He probably has a hand in everything worthwhile that comes on the Egyptian antiquities market."

Thierry said with a chuckle in his voice, "Sounds like he's the genie in the bottle, useful, but beware of the contents, it may be harmful." Everyone laughed at Thierry's remark that perhaps was true to the character of the mysterious Sheik Abdul Adin, we will have to wait and see, Pharrell quietly said to himself.

***

As Hugo and Pharrell passed through Bangkok passport control, Hugo caught sight of Ning who had patiently been waiting for their plane to arrive from France. Hugo embraced his partner, while Pharrell's thoughts were for Angelique; he wondered if Angelique had missed him as much he had missed the company of her. They decided to take a taxi together to their hotel, as Hugo had decided he would stay a night in Bangkok before driving the long distance north to his home. Hugo had told Pharrell on the plane his plans for the future. "It's time for younger blood, *mon cher ami*. I'm glad to be going home. The stress in this business is too much, for an old dog like me," Hugo had said to Pharrell.

That night Pharrell met with Angelique and the feelings for each other was evident for anyone to see. The sexual attraction had grown between them since their last time together. Pharrell noticed how his whole body lingered for her; he especially felt his trousers tighten from the arousal of Angelique's body close to his. He wondered if Angelique's body felt the same sexual awareness as they held hands under the table, as they sat there opposite Hugo and Ning in the restaurant, these were his thoughts.

Although Hugo was a master connoisseur of food, everyone decided that Ning should order the food. Pharrell and Angelique both thought Ning's choice of Thai dishes would surprise their taste buds, and Hugo already knew Ning was a great cook. "Let's raise a toast in be back home," Hugo said holding a glass of wine and waiting for everyone to do likewise and raise their glasses before continuing. "It's now time for Pharrell to take up the challenge," he roared.

"When do you plan to leave for Egypt?" Angelique whispered to Pharrell.

"Not sure. It depends on your plans. How are you riding a camel?" Pharrell replied to Angelique as everyone laughed at his remark. With a broad smile and in a jovial tone of voice he continued talking. "No, I'm serious; I would like you to come with me to Egypt. Can you come with me?

"Yes, I would like to come with you, but I cannot just drop everything and suddenly just go to some far flung place with you. Angelique had not told Pharrell who she really was, that would come in time, but, not know it was safer that way, she said to herself. "I fancy riding a camel at some point, it sounds like fun."

"Don't ask me…," Hugo roared with laughter and then said, "The poor camel wouldn't be able to take my weight."

Everyone laughed and Pharrell stood up and jokingly said, "Anyone for a camel ride!"

After everyone had finished laughing, Angelique then turned and faced Pharrell and asked in a serious tone of voice, "Do you think you will find what you are looking for in Egypt?"

Pharrell noticed the sharp tone in Angelique's voice and guessed that Angelique was probably hurting inside, he surmised. "I hope so. But, this quest has been ongoing for years for me. Over the years, I have been on a continually quest to find rare books and documents; it's my business, although I should stay in Norway more often. These days, my friend Joachim runs the book shop while I'm away. The power of the Internet and email etc…it's easy to stay in touch"

"Why is this book so important…the *Shahbla el Allah*?" Angelique asked.

Pharrell replied, "It's not that important. But, since, I first heard about the book I have been intrigued to find out more, and of course to find it, if possible. Let's not forget, that it's not a book in the modern sense of the word…as a book with hundreds of pages etc…it's most likely to be only a few sheets of papyrus. These documents of papyrus we refer to as a book. But, it's the legend that captivates my imagination…also the fact that it has been lost to history. And, is out there somewhere, waiting to be found and revealed to the world." Pharrell paused momentarily and saw the waitress approaching.

"Can I help you, sir?" the waitress asked.

Pharrell ordered another round of drinks and continued talking. "Yes…it's what's written in the *Shahbla el*

Allah that excites me, more than the quest of finding it."

Hugo said with seriousness in his voice, "You have to be careful you don't upset the religious community when you reveal these religious artefacts to the world. Remember, when they found the lost gospels of James and others recently…the current religious community basically dismissed the lost gospels as unimportant. Yet, the lost gospels gave a new interpretation of the life of Jesus and his followers…and the early days of Christianity."

"There is also the recent find in the 1990's of the lost gospel of Judas," Ning said with a soft tone in her voice as she tried to join the conversation.

"Ning is right. Archaeologists found the lost gospel of Judas in the Egyptian desert in the 90s. The text of the gospel was controversial because it stated that the betrayal of Jesus to the Romans was instigated by Jesus with the help of Judas Iscariot and not the way it is currently portrayed in the Bible," Hugo said with authority in his voice.

"The truth is often clouded by years of dust," Angelique said with sadness in her voice. "You grow-up believing something for years and then in a second it disappears."

"Sorry…I didn't mean to upset you, *ma cherie*," Hugo said with the look of shock on his face at what he had said had upset Angelique somehow.

"No, no…It's not your fault Hugo. You can't hide the truth for long. Going to Sunday school as a child you are taught one story and then you grow-up believing that story. You have a faith and you follow the story how it's told in the Bible, it's only when you realise that much of that story is false that you then question your beliefs and faith," Angelique said with a sadness in her voice clearly audible as she explained her disappointment of finding out some parts of the Bible differ completely from what she was taught at school.

"It happened to me too…this week…I found out that Darwin's theory has a lot of holes, it's riddled with them. I've had to question my beliefs since I started to ask the right questions. When you ask the right questions…Darwin's theory of evolution doesn't pan out. Even, today, the school system teaches the Darwin theory of evolution and forgets about all the problems that have been identified by current science," Pharrell said with an enthusiastic gesture with his hands.

"That's the problem with history, it's constantly being rewritten and analysed as new knowledge is found," Hugo stated with authority.

"Let's change the subject?" Ning asked.

"Let's have another round of drinks…I feel like celebrating?" Pharrell asked as he surveyed the busy restaurant and caught the eye of the waitress.

"What can I get you, sir," the waitress asked as she arched her head.

As Pharrell ordered the round of drinks he momentarily thought about what Professor Frieda Maupin had said to him about the *Special Event Theory*. He chewed the words over his tongue as he quietly repeated the sentence in his mind.

"What are we celebrating…Pharrell," Hugo asked.

"The *Special Event Theory*, the reason why we are all here, now! What Professor Frieda Maupin said the other day? Pharrell replied with excitement in his voice as he waited for everyone to raise their glass and toast the *Special Event Theory*. He felt like someone addicted to a drug, he had to find out more. It was part of his quest for some reason there must be a link, he was sure there was a link between the two.

"Oh…yes. The *Special Event Theory* is indeed more plausible every time I think about it. It's definitely worth celebrating." Hugo agreed.

"What is the *Special Event Theory*?" Angelique queried Hugo and Pharrell to explain.

"It's a theory that challenges the Darwinian theory of the evolution of Man," Pharrell replied.

"How does it challenge Darwin's theory?" Angelique asked briskly.

"What do you think, Hugo?" Pharrell enquired.

"Are you asking if I believe in the *Special Event Theory* or how it challenges Darwin's theory? It getting late and I don't have all night to explain what Professor Maupin said. But, essentially,…the Special Event occurred around forty to fifty thousand years ago. Around this time there would have been other species of hominid walking around at the same time as our ancestor…the hominid that evolved into Homo sapiens the present day man. Our species suddenly developed intelligence and we could describe intelligence as the ability to think ahead in simple terms. Now, you have to ask yourself at this point…why only our species? Why were we that special…as not forgetting we are only another species of animal? Around this time we started making tools…that is planning ahead…hence intelligence. Now, how, does this challenge Darwin's theory of evolution is the million dollar question and answer? According to Darwin in his theory of evolution by *natural selection*, a species evolves over a period of millions of years…tens of millions…hundreds of millions of years, essentially a very long time. Suddenly, as a species Man has intelligence…virtually overnight in evolutionary terms. So, can you see how this challenges Darwin's theory?" Hugo replied.

"That was great Hugo…I would have struggled to explain the essence of the issue as well as you have," Pharrell said in a tone of voice that had a real honesty in its conviction.

"It's time we started heading back to our hotel," Hugo said.

After saying their goodbyes Pharrell and Angelique waved through the rear window of their taxi. Pharrell decided to ask Angelique if she felt like sharing the bed. They agreed to go back to Angelique's hotel room for the evening. "Are you sure, you want to do this? Pharrell asked. "Yes, of course. I've been frisky since you mentioned riding a camel!" Angelique replied with a cute smile on her face.

It had been a long time for both of them since they last had sex. The initial slow caressing and fondling turned into a frenetic few minutes of ecstasy. Pharrell had breathed a sigh of relief when he realised Angelique had had a full organism at the same time he ejaculated. He felt the comfort of her body against his, the warmth of her body, the perfume he would not forget. They both fell asleep in each other's arms. In the morning they had sex again, it just happened naturally without any conversation.

***

"Goodbye, Angelique. I will phone you as soon as I can," Pharrell said his parting words like a man with a new zest for life. He felt happy inside, the first time he felt the confidence of being in love. He heard the sound of the phone line disconnecting above the sound of a busy airport as he waited to go through Egyptian passport control. He had landed in Egypt hoping to find the mysterious Sheik Abdul Adin the Egyptian art dealer. Lucy Bouchard had said the Sheik would know everything worth knowing in the Egyptian art market, but finding him would be difficult because the Sheik dealt in the underworld of the black market in ancient Egyptian artefacts, but he had to find the Sheik somehow, he said to himself.

"Can I help you, sir," the taxi driver said.

You know when you are in a third world country, the taxi drivers get out of their vehicles and tout for business face to face. And, today was no exception, Pharrell thought. Pharrell could see the melee of taxi drivers, taxis, and people trying hard to avoid each other. The first breath of Egyptian air he could feel the heat inside his mouth and taste the pollution from the vehicles coming and going from the busy airport arrivals area. The diminutive figure dressed in black touting for his business wasted no time grabbing his luggage before he was being ushered into the back seat of his dusty old ford saloon.

Pharrell said, "Take to me to Hotel El Toro."

"Yes, sir, Hotel El Toro," the taxi driver said. "My name is Mahmoud. Call me Mahmoud, I find places you want to go, sir. Call my number; I take you where you want to go anytime, day or night. Here's my card, call me first. I have big family to feed, need your business, sir. I find all the best places to visit in Cairo. My family have lived in Cairo…for long time. Call me…Mahmoud."

"Yes okay, Mahmoud, I will call you." Pharrell said hoping the taxi driver would stop talking without committing, in his mind, to his extensive offer. Perhaps, the taxi driver knows the Sheik's whereabouts, Pharrell wondered. "Do you know how I can find Sheik Abdul Adin? The Sheik is an art dealer. Do you understand…he buys and sells ancient Egyptian artefacts?"

"Yes, he is well known in Egypt...Sheik Abdul Adin...the 'Thief of Baghdad'," Mahmoud said with the enthusiasm of a prophet preaching to the faithful followers.
"Why do you call him the 'Thief of Baghdad', has he...?"
Mahmoud was quick to reply before Pharrell had had time to finish what he had to say. "It is said, that he bought the stolen contents of the Baghdad national museum for, how you say...pennies."
"You mean when the American army entered Baghdad during the Iraqi war?"
"Yes, sir, the Iraq war...the museum was destroyed by the locals. Bad people...bad people take from the museum and sell on the black market."
"Do you know where I can find **Sheik Abdul Adin?**" Pharrell asked not expecting a positive reply.
"No...No sir, the 'thief of Baghdad' is wanted by the government. He is wanted by the Police."
"Okay, Mahmoud...how far to hotel?"
"Not far, sir...five minutes." Mahmoud replied remonstrating with his raised hand and splaying his five fingers.
As the taxi wound its way around the streets of Cairo, Pharrell observed the street traders trying to sell their tourist wares, from moveable carts the smell of food cooking would occasionally sweep an aroma through the taxi window along with a cool breeze that smelt sweet to him, but probably tasted like the hottest spiciest dish you can buy, he mused.

***

"You are the guide?" Pharrell asked.
"Yes, sir, my name is Mohamed," the Arab replied bowing his head.

"Where are your camels?"

"Over there, by the water hole, they will not stray far…they are camels. They do what you want…go far they will, my camels," Mohamed muttered.

Pharrell could see a group of men and camels gathered round the edges of the natural spring. Mature palm trees surrounded the spring providing much needed shade from the punishing heat of the sun for the men and camels. The Arab men paid no attention to the foreigner they were too busy enjoying the charms of the oasis.

"Where do you want to go…I take you all over Egypt?" Mohamed asked.

"I understand you know how to get to St Anthony's Monastery, is that so?"

The Arab gestured with his head and said, "Yes sir, we leave early in the morning. Before the sun burns the desert. But first, we will camp here and prepare for the desert cold that can kill a man before the sun rises and warms the blood of men."

The Arab shouted to the other Bedouin Arabs and a scurry of activity saw the arrival of the sunset as the flames of the camp fire began to warm Pharrell as he stood there watching the men he had hired to take him to the legendary monastery. An early Christian monastery dating from the first century A.D. and only accessible via the use of camels to climb the mountain passes as the only road nearby was approximately ten kilometres away. He felt confident riding with these Bedouin guides, his only doubts were his thoughts about Angelique.

It was a clear night, the cosmos revealed its beauty. The Milky Way was visible, and for the first time Pharrell could see its majestic beauty without the light pollution he had experienced all his life in Norway, and indeed many other parts of the world he had visited. His immediate thoughts were of the ancient Sumerians and the Babylonians who were masters of the night's sky. Those early astrologers knew more about the cosmos in many different ways they were far ahead of their time, and for a few moments his mind travelled the cosmos.

Mohamed gestured and said, "Sit down, and eat, sir."

For a few moments, Pharrell had drifted into a different realm. The magic of seeing the beauty of the visible cosmos had transfixed his thoughts into a time and place where the origin of the legend he was chasing started. An open fire under the night's sky had a kind of spiritual awareness on his thoughts; he could see why the early astrologers and their populace were also transfixed by the cosmos.

"Do you like our food?"

Pharrell replied, "Yes, it's good, it warms you against the desert cold. I can feel the heat building."

"That's good, sir. The spices warm your blood, its helps to keep the cold from your bones. The Bedouin have used these spices for thousands of years. We are like our camels we know how to survive the desert night and day. This monastery you want to visit, why do want to visit this place?"

Pharrell thought for several minutes before answering this direct question. He considered the Arabs as a people who are never afraid to be polite when it came to knowing your business. "I would like to read their library of books. I am a book collector." Pharrell replied with the authority and honesty like a judge summing up a case in a court of law.

Pharrell noticed the flames of the fire began to flicker in violet schisms. "The wind is getting stronger," he said as the cold began to bite the cheeks of his face.

"Yes sir. That is the Levant," Mohamed said.

"The Levant...is that what you said? What is this word Levant?" Pharrell asked wanting to know more.

"It comes from the east of the Mediterranean Sea. This wind is well known in the desert, so we call it Levant. The wind, that comes from the east. Our brothers pray to the east, so the wind has many legends to tell. The wind originates in a land we call Levant, it's roughly bounded on the north by the mountains of Taurus, and on the south by the Arabian Desert, and on the west by the Mediterranean Sea, while on the east it extends towards the Zagros Mountains."

"You have a good understanding of English. How did you learn such good English?"

"You have to understand that I am not a Bedouin Arab, my family comes from Syria where I attended university and learnt my English there, before I decided to live a life as a Bedouin Arab. I was born in Aleppo that was the second largest city in Syria until the Middle East Spring and the uprising brought only misery for so many people, including my family."

Mohamed then went quiet as the desert wind swirled around the camp fire. Pharrell felt the chill and the heat of the fire at the same time. Pharrell's back braced the cold and his face the glowing warmth from the fire as he reflected on what Mohamed had said. Pharrell looked at Mohamed's face and saw the tears that wanted to break upon his face, but were held back for another time, when he was alone without the other Arabs around the camp fire looking on, he surmised.

Pharrell momentarily thought about the loss he had suffered as a child when his grandfather had died. He still had the pain of that loss, and realised that his parents were wrong to shelter him from death and he remembered his parent's insistence that he should not attend his grandfather's funeral. When one loves someone the loss of that person or persons can be too much to bear and we should never hide the tears for them.

"There is a legend that comes from the time of the first prophet," Mohamed said as he looked up to stars in the night's sky. "Would you like to hear it?"

"Yes, of course. Please tell," Pharrell retorted.

Mohamed took a sip from his cup of the black coffee and cleared his throat from the desert sand the wind had brought. "One day a man was walking through the desert and came upon a rabbit."

Pharrell noticed a smile creep upon Mohamed's face as he continued with the story. Perhaps Mohamed told the story to all the foreigners he met guiding them throughout the Egyptian desert, he mused.

The rabbit said to the man, "Where do you go?" As Mohamed spoke his voice took on a mystical association.

The man replied, "I go to seek my fortune."

"Fortune...what fortune?" the rabbit asked.

"The treasure of Asqanu, on the Mediterranean coast," the man replied.

"Will you take me with you? I know this place," the rabbit said.

"What good is a talking rabbit?" the man asked.

The rabbit replied, "What good is it that you are lost?"

The rabbit then said, "Man thinks, just because he can talk that he is smarter than the rabbit, but forgets he is an animal who is lost."

"What do you think, the moral of the story relates to? Mohamed asked inquisitively.

Pharrell thought for a moment and considered the question. "Where is this place...Asqanu? Is it a real place?

"Yes, of course. Today, it is called Ashkelon a city not far from Gaza on the Mediterranean coast in Israel," Mohamed replied.

Pharrell nodded his head with agreement and said, "I'm not sure what the story or legend is trying to teach, or indeed, the moral of the legend. But, like all legends there are usually some truths in the story."

Mohamed then explained to Pharrell the moral of the legend. The moral he said teaches us to beware of the dangers of the desert. Mohamed emphasised that you can easily get lost in the desert, and perhaps your only savour will be to remember this legend before embarking on a trek across the desert.

"Who was the first prophet?"

Mohamed replied, "Most people believe the prophet Amos, although there were many prophets at this time."

Pharrell was intrigued to know what Mohamed knew about the prophet Amos. "I don't think I have heard of Amos before; tell me...what do you know about the prophet Amos?"

"He was the first prophet to make a prophecy about the destruction of Israel." Before continuing Mohamed looked around like a man who was lost. Perhaps tomorrow or the day after a sand storm would come, he said to himself.

"Amos saw the future destruction of Israel as a consequence of God's wrath at the people of Israel continued idolatry of other Gods. It is said the message Amos received was from God. And it is said that he pleaded with God to save Israel; but God chose to teach the Israelites a lesson for their idolatry for other Gods. The Israelites had broken the covenant Moses had made with God. At that time the Israelites worshipped many Gods, these Gods were associated with paganism. At

that time, the Jewish religion had not established itself as the dominant religion in Israel."
"Do you believe this legend?"
Mohamed chuckled and took a sip of his coffee before replying to Pharrell's question. Mohamed looking at Pharrell and remonstrating with his hands he replied, "Look at the night sky you can see countless stars in our universe all waiting to be discovered some day. We should have no doubts about life on other planets. It's just a legend to teach the importance of valuing other creatures and to be careful not to stray into the desert without understanding its dangers."

***

The noise of people talking broke Pharrell's dream inside the tent and he awoke to find Mohamed already preparing some hot coffee. Pharrell could hear only the faintest ruffle of the canvas tent amongst the muffled sound of voices outside the tent. The wind must have died during the night, he mused.
"What time is it," Pharrell asked. And immediately realised it was a stupid question to ask Mohamed.
"We don't need the assistance of a wristwatch out here in the desert. The day and night is our only guide. The Bedouin have survived here in the desert for thousands of years without the need for a watch. But, today many Bedouin have succumbed to this piece of technology. Personally, I owe one, but prefer not to wear a watch."
Mohamed paused briefly to chuckle and then said, "Besides, out here in the desert where are you going to go…nowhere fast, that's for sure. What is the point of knowing the time if you are dying of thirst? It's like finding a fortune on an island, only to find you are alone with nowhere to go and without the possibility of

rescue. Your ownership of a watch has no value in the desert."

Pharrell took a slurp of hot coffee from his cup and nodded his head in agreement and said, "It sounds like the wind has died down."

"Yes sir, the Levant comes and goes, but it will be back with vengeance in a day or so, you wait and see," Mohamed said with the authority of experience in his voice. "I just hope we can avoid a sand storm before we reach the monastery."

"You believe there is a sand storm coming then?" Pharrell asked in a concerned manner in his voice and with a frown visible across his forehead.

Mohamed replied, "Yes, usually, after the Levant we can expect a sand storm. The Levant is a sign to signal an approaching storm. The Bedouin swear by the wind that comes from the east."

As the caravan departed from the shelter of the small oasis Pharrell could still see the stars in the sky and the briefest glimpse on the horizon of the approaching sunrise. It was still cold the sun had not begun to heat the desert to a blazing furnace that would come later when the sun was at its zenith at midday. Pharrell's camel was surprisingly comfortable to ride. Angelique would have enjoyed the experience of riding a camel through the desert. Perhaps, someday he would return to Egypt with Angelique and view the ancient temples and pyramids on the back of camels together, he mused. Mohamed had told him that all the camels have names and the one he was riding was called Jazmin because it had a pleasant smell and was also a female.

It was several hours since leaving the oasis and for most of the way the caravan of camels and riders made its way over and between sand dunes that stretched to the distant horizon and to the west an outline of mountain tops pierced the horizon only visible from the top of some of the highest sand dunes.

Pharrell had wondered briefly how Mohamed and the Bedouin knew which way to go in the desert, but soon realised they must use the sun and desert features like the mountains to guide them. It was surprisingly simple to work out how the Bedouin navigate the journey when you think about the question for long enough.

It was late afternoon when the wind started to strengthen. As each hour passed Pharrell felt the wind on his face getting stronger and colder. In the distance over the horizon the clouds had turned black as if it was about to rain with rage.

"We need to camp here, near that outcrop of rock," Mohamed said.

"It looks like a storm is coming our way," Pharrell replied.

"Yes, but it's not a storm like you expect. In the distance you can just see the beginning of a sand storm. We will pitch the tent in the *wadi* below those rocks for protection against the sand. The camels will be protected and our tents will be below most of the wind."

"You think it's a sand storm then?" Pharrell asked.

"Yes, most definitely…when the Levant comes it precedes a sand storm; otherwise, the wind blows from the west off the Mediterranean coast. The wind that blows from that direction is always warm and often brings rain, whereas, the Levant wind is cooler and brings a companion sand storm," Mohamed said with the authority of experience in his voice.

"Will there be time to prepare some food and hot coffee," Pharrell asked intently.

"Yes, we have about one to two hours before the full force of the sand storm reaches us here. Once, we have securely pitched the tents and anchored the camels down we can eat and drink inside the tent. We are lucky this *wadi* is here, otherwise, we would be at the mercy of the sand storm. Many people die in these sand storms, mostly, because they get lost and eventually die of thirst in the desert. The sand can strip the skin from your face and blind your eyes before you have time to find cover from the sand storm."

Pharrell could hear the rustle of the wind outside the tent, the tremendous gusts at times shook the tent violently as he and the Arabs ate their food and drank their coffee trying to avoid the chaos outside by the constant chatter amongst themselves, occasionally, the chatter went quiet, momentarily, as another strong gust of wind shook the tent and everyone looked at each other in shock.

"How long will the sand storm last?" Pharrell asked Mohamed.

"Until the early hours of tomorrow, most likely by sunrise…the storm will have gone further west or completely abated. But, a sand storm will come again in a few days' time. Perhaps, we can avoid the next one, who knows," Mohamed replied.

"I hope you are right. I would hate to get caught in another sand storm."

Mohamed described to Pharrell that the Bedouin were used to the desert, for them it's natural and they regard these events such as sand storms as part of the cycle of life. Its nature's way that the soil and sand that gets blown away eventually ends up in another part of the world, where the dust will help make the land fertile and prosperous for those farmers in distant corners of the world. Pharrell listened intently.

"Yes, I have heard this is true, apparently, the dust from sand storms in the Sahara reach as far as the American continent," Pharrell remarked.

Mohamed nodded his head in agreement and momentarily spoke in Arabic to his fellow companions who immediately stopped their chatter to listen to his words. "I will now tell you a story." Mohamed then spoke in Arabic and then told Pharrell that he would translate into English for his benefit.

Mohamed began telling the story in Arabic and Pharrell eagerly waited for the English translation. "The story begins where my ancestors were born in the land between two rivers, the land they called Mesopotamia, that is now part of Iraq and Syria," Mohamed said before pausing to speak in Arabic again.

The wind shook the tent again violently and everyone looked startled before Mohamed continued telling his story. "One day a young prince was travelling through his father's kingdom and he was alone except for his personal servant and he came across an old man being led by a donkey. At first, the young prince did not notice the old man was blind. The old man asked the prince if he could travel together because he said the journey was long, and he had only the donkey to talk to. The prince granted the old man his wish and they continued together on their journey," Mohamed paused before repeating the translation in Arabic to his Arab comrades eagerly waiting for more of the story. Their eyes were glued to Mohamed's demeanour like a tiger stalking its prey.

While Pharrell watched Mohamed speak in Arabic his thoughts were of Angelique and how she would have enjoyed this adventure into the Egyptian desert. What she was doing right now in Thailand? Perhaps, she was thinking about him, he mused.

A strange whirling sound could be heard outside as the sand storm continued its path across the land. "After a short distance, the prince asked the old man why he was walking instead of riding the donkey. The old man replied that the donkey was old like him and was already laden with all his possessions. So the prince instructed his servant to transfer the old man's possessions to the servant's camel. This way the old man could ride his donkey and keep up with the prince and his servant on their camels. The old man thanked the prince for this gesture and all three of them continued on their journey," Mohamed said while occasionally pausing to catch his breath and see the reaction from his captive audience.

Again Mohamed paused and repeated the story so far in Arabic to his fellow Arabs. Then he continued the story in English. "They say that the wind brings the souls of the dead to life for all those that have lost their lives in the desert. The desert wind sings for all the lost souls who become lost in the desert. As the trio continued their journey a cool wind became stronger as each hour passed, until they saw the first sign of a dust cloud in the distance. The old man said to the prince that they should make camp and find some shelter from the impending sand storm. The prince had grown up within his father's palace and had had no experience of the desert. Also, the prince was not used to taking advice from lowly subjects of his father's kingdom. So the prince continued with his journey with his servant and the old man as there were many hours before the sunset." Mohamed paused again to repeat what he had just said in Arabic.

The noise from the wind outside sometimes drowned out the voice of Mohamed, so Pharrell had to purposely make an effort to hear what he was saying by leaning forward and closer to Mohamed. "It was not long before the sand storm caught the trio out in the open without any protection from the piercing sand. During this mayhem the prince was lost and so was his servant and they were never seen again. The old man survived the storm with his donkey and was able to tell the story, but he had lost all of his possessions," Mohamed said before translating the last part of the story to his fellow Arabs.

"So do you see the moral of the story, sir?" Mohamed asked turning his head away from his fellow Arabs and he looked straight into Pharrell's eyes that looked at first startled. Pharrell again regained his composure and said, "Yes, I believe I do."

Mohamed said, "Good, it's now time to sleep. If you can...we have a long journey tomorrow and we leave early, before the sun rises."

"You are right about that...if you can sleep...because the noise of the wind outside is enough to make an insomniac sleepless for obvious reasons."

"You need to drink some of the local liquid...we call it *alga rah*, sir."

"What is this drink made from? Pharrell asked Mohamed.

"Look around sir what do you see outside, if you were outside at this moment?"

"All I can see is miles and miles of sand and a few scrubs of plant life scattered amongst the dunes." Pharrell replied.

"No sir, you have not fully opened your eyes, yes, you can see the sand of the desert, but you forget about us... and more important are the camels. The drink is matured in a special way from the camels' milk. And, in particular the camel you are riding, you see it provides most of the milk we need," Mohamed said.

Pharrell was embarrassed not to have thought about the camels. He smiled at Mohamed and realised he had learnt a valuable lesson. "Of course, I missed it, the camels' milk. Well, I will try some, if it helps me sleep through this storm."

"Of course, sir, I will prepare some for you."

Pharrell watched Mohamed as he heated a pan with some of the milk over the hot stones that they had heated earlier that day outside in the camp fire to heat the milk inside the tent. These stones were not just any odd stones; they were oval in shape and blackened from many fires. The Arabs were certainly industrious people, he thought.

"Here, drink this sir."

Pharrell took the cup from Mohamed and then took a sniff of the hot camel's milk. It smelt okay to Pharrell, as he took a hesitant slurp. After few more mouthfuls of camels' milk Pharrell was ready to sleep and had begun to dream.

***

"Wake up, wake up, sir," Mohamed shouted.

Pharrell had awaked from his sleep and could hear immediately the commotion from outside the tent. Mohamed was leaning over him as Pharrell opened his eyes. At first, Pharrell was startled, but soon his eyes adjusted to the light as he saw the familiar face of Mohamed staring at him.

"We have prepared some food outside by the camp fire. In the meantime, gather your things, so we can drop the tent and make our way to the monastery."

As Pharrell sat by the camp fire he watched as the Arabs dismantled the tent and packed the camels ready for the day ahead. Mohamed was busy giving orders to the other Bedouin Arabs. The sun was already beginning to appear on the horizon. Pharrell noticed the sand dunes looked impressive against the shadows of the rising sun.

"Are you ready, sir?" Mohamed asked Pharrell as Mohamed deadened the camp fire with his feet. The sand soon covered the flames and was out.

"When do you think we will arrive at the monastery?" Pharrell asked.

"Hopefully, God willing before sunset," Mohamed replied.

The caravan of Arabs and Pharrell mounted their camels and were on their way into the desert for the third day. Pharrell's thoughts were of Angelique. He wondered what she was doing and how she would have enjoyed his adventure in the desert. Did she feel the say way as he did, he whispered to himself.

***

"Hello, Mr. Lebervitz...its Jac."

"Go ahead, tell me what you have found out..," Harry asked bluntly has ever.

No time for pleasantries, Jac thought, before business that was Harry Lebervitz. "The French Antique and Antiquities Police Force were following Hugo and Pharrell because they were seen in Algiers in the company of a known suspect dealing in stolen artefacts associated with Egypt. Namely, the fall of Saddam Hussein in the Iraq war, when their national museum of antiquities In Baghdad was ransacked."

"Who was the dealer?" Harry asked impatiently.

"He is a Russian called Oleg Dimitrov, who is associated with an Egyptian dealer named as Sheik Adbul Adin, also known as the 'Thief of Baghdad'."

"This is good work. What else have you found out?"

"The French police have been working with the Egyptian authorities and the Iraqi government since the fall of Saddam Hussein's government to retrieve artefacts stolen from their national museum and return them to Iraq. It seems most of the artefacts stolen from the Iraqi national museum have found their way onto the black market in Egypt and other countries."

"Do the French police mention the papyri I bought from Hugo and Pharrell?" Harry asked.

"No, according to my sources there was some sort of mix-up at the airport and there was no one to question their stay in Algiers. According to my sources the police have no idea what they bought or if they bought anything from the Russian in Algiers. This is good news… is it not for you, Mr. Lebervitz?" Jac asked.

Jac could hear the sound of a grumble down the phone. And it was a few seconds before Harry replied to Jac's question.

"Have you anymore information for me?"

"No, that's it for now…what do you want me to do?" Jac asked.

"Find out what you can on the Egyptian dealer…the one they call the 'Thief of Baghdad'. I want you to catch a flight to Cairo tomorrow, but first, be here tomorrow morning at 9.am in the hotel reception area. Is that understood?" Harry asked.

"Yes." The phone line disconnected. That was typical of Mr Lebervitz, no time for pleasantries, Jac said to himself.

***

Angelique was at the border between Myanmar and Thailand waiting for the truck carrying the guns to arrive.

"Hello sir, currently waiting for the *dragons* to arrive, any news?" Angelique asked, using her encrypted mobile phone line. "The *dragons* are due to pass through within the next thirty minutes, will observe and follow at a distance, sir."

"Okay, current Intel…Thai drug lords need those *dragons*. Find out and report…ASAP?" the section head said, before the call was disconnected.

***

Pharrell noticed that apart from the desert vultures circling above and the odd screech from the birds the desert was calm without the slightness hint of a cool breeze. Even with most of his face covered with an Arab *shemagh* to protect him from the scorching sun, he still felt the occasional drop of sweat from his brow work its way down his neck scarf into his wet from sweat shirt. If Jochim in Norway was right, this journey to find this monastery would be the best chance of finding a long lost manuscript and perhaps more, the days had long gone when you could buy treasure for peanuts. The modernisation of Egypt with easy transport links such as motorways and railroads had made it easy for any aspiring treasure seeker to search the libraries of early Christian monasteries, most of the oldest Christian monasteries were now so accessible that they had become tourist attractions and were unlikely to hold the kind of treasure or information Pharrell was seeking.

"How far is it to the monastery Mohamed?" Pharrell shouted to Mohamed, who was riding ahead of the caravan.

Pharrell noticed Mohamed raise his arm and show one finger, and he assumed Mohamed meant one hour. He hoped it meant one hour although the hours had passed quickly since they started their journey, he had time to think about Angelique and perhaps their future together married with children.

On the horizon Pharrell saw the valley ahead and for the first time caught a glimpse of a giant cross the shimmered against the sun's rays. The monastery was still a considerable distance away, but, at least, he could see the dome that supported the cross above the monastery, he somehow felt welcome. He could feel the attraction of the cross and how those early Christians would have been drawn by its presence in the bleakness of the desert.

As the caravan got closer and closer to the monastery the sun was already beginning its downward fall towards the distant horizon. The rectangular outer walls and the inner buildings could be clearly seen as the caravan made its way down into the valley where the monastery was protected on three sides by a range of steep rocky cliffs. Anyone approaching the monastery would be seen well before they reached the doors of the monastery.

Pharrell saw the silhouette of a person standing by the entrance to the monastery, and he wondered if it was the priest he had spoken to over the phone several days before.

"Welcome, my friends," the person shouted out.

The caravan stopped in front of the main gates to the entrance of the monastery. The gates had already been opened and the caravan was led inside by the priest to an extensive courtyard. Immediately, several of the inhabitants of the monastery gathered round to greet the caravan.

Pharrell could hear several different languages being spoken, mostly Aramaic, he thought.

"You must be Mr. Anderson?" said the priest.

"Yes. Please call me Pharrell."

"Father Dimitros is waiting for you. Did you bring the goods we asked for?" The priest asked.

"Yes, of course. Speak to Mohamed. He will arrange for the goods to be unloaded. Look over there, Mohamed is the one giving orders to the other Arabs," Pharrell said, as he pointed with his arm out-stretched at Mohamed.

The priest spoke with Mohamed and arranged for the goods they had brought to be unloaded. "You can camp here in the courtyard if you wish," the priest said to Mohamed.

"Thank you, for your offer, but we are Bedouin and prefer to camp outside. Besides our camels will make a mess of your courtyard if you let them stay here," Mohamed said.

"I understand what you mean, but you are welcome to stay here if you change your mind."

The priest then asked, "What about you Mr. Anderson…we can arrange a room for you?"

"No thank you, I have got used to sleeping in a tent and besides if I sleep in a comfortable bed for a few nights then on my journey back I will need to get used to sleeping in a tent again. So, thanks again for the offer," Pharrell replied.

"Okay, I understand. Come with me and I will take you to see Father Dimitros."

As Pharrell followed the priest across the courtyard and into the monastery he noticed how well kept the building was. He noticed how the stone floors were clean from dust and sand from the desert. Some of the walls were clad with white painted plaster, but most walls were bare stone and the roofs of the buildings were clad with clay shingles that had weathered with the sun and the desert wind and turned them into a brownish colour. The monastery was first built around the fourth century Joachim had told him and before this early Christians had settled there for perhaps hundreds of years before establishing a monastery. The location of the monastery was certainly inaccessible even today; you could see why the early Christians built there monastery here far away from people, he mused.

Pharrell followed the priest up the stairs leading onto a balcony with rooms on one side and a view onto the courtyard on the other side. Pharrell caught a glimpse of Mohamed and his fellow Arabs unloading the goods in the courtyard Father Dimitros had requested. At the end of the balcony the priest knocked on the door and they both entered the room.

"This is Father Dimitros, Mr Anderson. Will you need me?" The priest asked.

"No, you may go Peter," Father Dimitros said, as Peter bowed his head and closed the door.

"Welcome Mr. Anderson to our monastery. Have you had a pleasant journey?"

Pharrell noticed that Father Dimitros was tall lean man as he stood up from behind his desk to shake heads. His piercing blue eyes and a roman shaped nose and a grey wiry moustache and beard that complimented his shaven balding head were distinctive, he thought. "Yes, better than I expected. Riding a camel for several days has been more comfortable than I expected. The only problem I had was sleeping through the desert storm the other night, but with the help of some camel's milk I was able to sleep through the storm," Pharrell replied.

"Did you bring the goods I requested?"

"Yes, of course. Everything you requested," Pharrell replied.

"The reason why I asked you to bring those supplies is because our usual person who supplies us is at present too ill to travel. And we don't get many visitors out here except the occasional pilgrims and of course people like you."

Pharrell looked straight into the eyes of Father Dimitros and wondered what he meant by his last comment. "What do you mean…people like me?" Pharrell asked, with a smile and a soft tone of voice.

"Over the years with have had a few collectors…or should I say treasure seekers. They come and go. They come here hoping to find a lost treasure hidden within our library and when they find what they're looking for they want to pay little more than grains of sand," Father Dimitros said in cordially manner already establishing the rules of the bargaining game with Pharrell.

"Can we offer you a room to sleep tonight?"

"No, but thanks for the offer…I have already explained to Peter that its better I sleep with my companions in the tent, it's something I have got used to on the journey here," Pharrell replied.

"How long are you planning to stay Mr. Anderson?"

"It all depends on how long it takes to go through your library, but two or three days at most. Besides, my companions need a rest before we journey back again, I'm sure," Pharrell replied.

"Good, let me show you our library and introduce you to Father Antonio, who looks after the library and who has a boundless knowledge you will find useful during your stay with us. Tonight, you and your companions are welcome to eat with us. We welcome the prospect of enlightened conversation," Father Dimitros said.

"Yes, of course…thank you for the offer."

"Good, follow me...our library is situated in the main tower where the room receives plenty of daylight and one can read and relax without distractions."

Father Dimitros led the way across the balcony overlooking the courtyard and around the corner up a stairway leading to the library. As Father Dimitros and Pharrell entered the library Father Antonio was kneeling busy carefully cleaning the dust from the books upon the lower wooden shelves that stretched all around the room from the floor to just above the height of the doorway. Father Antonio placed his round rimmed spectacles upon his head before offering his hand to Pharrell.

"This is Mr. Pharrell Anderson. Mr. Anderson this is Father Antonio, who will help you search our library," Father Dimitros said.

"Please call me by my first name," Pharrell said, as he shook hands with Father Antonio.

Pharrell noticed that Father Antonio was small in stature and completely bald hiding his true age. His deep brown eyes and roman shape nose combined with his Mediterranean complexion suited his chubby body. He was probably Greek or Italian, Pharrell said to himself.

"Please excuse me. I have to attend to some important business. I will leave you now in the capable hands of Father Antonio and see you and your companions later," Father Dimitros said.

"Of course...and thanks again Father Dimitros for letting me visit your beautiful monastery and view your library," Pharrell said, as Father Dimitros nodded his head in approval before leaving the room.

"Now, how can I assist you Mr. Anderson?" Father Antonio asked.

"Please call me Pharrell, I insist. Show me where you keep all of the earliest books, manuscripts or codices you have," Pharrell replied.

"We have some very old books, *et cetera*, but they are arranged and stored on the shelves in their relative subject. This library is used by all the priests, and so the subjects are varied from religion to philosophy and also some fiction. Sometimes a good novel to read is one way to fall asleep."

"Okay, what do you consider to be your oldest book here," Pharrell asked.

Father Antonio pointed to the corner of the room. "Over here we have an early Christian Bible dating from the fourth century and also many manuscripts dating from that period. I suggest you take a seat at one of the desks and I will bring you some books to get started. In the meantime, we can talk about your quest."

Pharrell was momentarily surprised and asked, "How did you know I was on a quest?"

"Simple my son, why else would you want to be here. You are searching for something like those that have been here before searching for treasure. Tell me Pharrell what your quest is for and, perhaps, I can help you," Father Antonio asked.

Pharrell looked at Father Antonio and smiled into his face and said, "I am a dealer of antiquarian books, manuscripts, and I travel the world looking for stock for my shop in Norway. But, you are right. I'm on a quest to find *the Shahbla el Allah* made famous by the ancient Babylonians. Have you heard about the *Shahbla el Allah*?" Pharrell asked.

"Yes, I have heard of this book, but you will not find that book here in our library," Father Antonio replied.

"Yes, I know that…but you asked me what my quest was and I told you."

"So, why come here to this monastery?" Father Antonio asked inquisitively shrugging his shoulders.

"Like I said, I buy and sell antiquarian books and manuscripts. So, I thought a visit to the monastery perhaps would prove rewarding."

"Yes, I understand. But why here...there are many cities in Egypt and also many bookshops and antique shops, which you could find more rewarding.... than this monastery. Besides, I don't think Father Dimitros would sell any of these old books, unless, it involved a large sum of money."

"You are right...there is more? I purposely chose this monastery or should I say my friend Joachim who manages my shop in Norway chose this monastery. We felt this monastery had the best prospect of...as they say...hidden treasure, because of its location...as you say...off the beaten track. The monastery is far from any roads and so not accessible for the average tourist," Pharrell replied.

"You are half right, but also half wrong. Yes, we don't get tourists unless they are lost. But, the determined adventurer, well, that's a different matter. Over the years we have had many such people like you, who come here hoping to find some sort of hidden treasure. These days many go away disappointed because all our treasures have been sold previously and now what is here in our library is not for sale, unless Father Dimitros has a change of heart."

"I guess it all depends on how much money is involved," Pharrell said.

Father Antonio laughed and said, "You are wrong again. Father Dimitros and indeed all the priests here care little for money. Yes, we need money to buy supplies *et cetera*, but we live a frugal life and we are largely self-sufficient with our fruit and vegetable garden combined with the livestock we keep. Besides, we receive regular donations from patrons all around the world, which is sufficient for our needs."

"Tell me what you know about the *Shahbla el Allaha*?" Pharrell asked wanting to change the subject of the conversation.

"Not much I can tell you that you probably already know," Father Antonio replied pausing briefly to hand another book to Pharrell. "Here take a look at this one. It's a book about alchemy…an early book…date unknown, but it's an interesting read. Quite amazing what these alchemists tried to do. The search for the philosopher's stone…changes base metals into silver and gold - a quest much like yours."

"What do you mean?" Pharrell asked curiously poised like a schoolboy eager to learn more from his teacher.

"The elixir for eternal life is another one that man has in the past tried to find. The *Shahbla el Allah* is another…a legend told by generation to generation through the ages. A myth, handed down through the ages, from father to son. Then the legend is written down, by an ancient scribe, who then embellishes it with their own ideas, and so on and on."

"So, you don't believe in the legend?"

Father Antonio looked straight into Pharrell's eyes and shrugged his shoulders and said, "No, because I believe in something else more powerful. So, until a scholar or scholars provide proof of its existence it's just a legend."

"But isn't most of what we know about the past a matter of blind faith?" Pharrell asked mawkishly not trying to invoke an argument about religion.

As Father Antonio was about to reply a loud bell rang out. "Aarrhh. It's time for me to get ready for supper, and, also for you and your companions. We will continue our conversation later. Let's go from here!"

As Pharrell approached the tent outside the wall of the monastery he was greeted by Mohamed with open arms and a wide grin across his face.

"Greetings, sir, I understand we have been invited to eat with the monks in the monastery. We are ready and wait for you," Mohamed said.

"You can go ahead and I will follow shortly. I have some notes to make before I forget them," Pharrell said.

"No, sir, we wait for you. It would not be right to go ahead without you. After all, you are the reason we are here. Did you find what you are looking for in the library?" Mohamed asked inquisitively.

Pharrell paused momentarily before answering such a direct question, and wondered why Mohamed was again asking questions about his business. Pharrell decided to ignore Mohamed's question and decided to reply with a question of his own. "How long will it take us to reach *Zafarana*?" Without waiting for a reply Pharrell had sat down inside the tent and began to make his notes of what he had learned that day so far.

"Around two days maybe more. Why do you ask?"

Pharrell mumbled something and continued writing his notes; he had already decided not to answer the question at that time. "Okay, I have finished my notes. So we can go now and eat with the monks."

As Pharrell and his Arab companions made the way inside the monastery they were greeted by Father Antonio who led the way.

"I hope you enjoy our hospitality tonight Mr Anderson. But, please remember this is not a hotel so our food, perhaps, will not be up to the standards you are used to."

"Don't worry Father Antonio, I have stayed in many hotels where the food was at best the least of my problems," Pharrell said with a wry smile.

As Father Antonio led the way they were joined by other priests into a room with several wooden dining tables and wooden benches, some of the priests were already waiting for Pharrell and his companions to arrive. Pharrell could see Father Dimitros standing talking with other priests as they entered the room.

"Please take a seat," Father Dimitros said as Pharrell and his companions were shown where to sit.

"We will now pray for the food we are about to receive," Father Dimitros said.

As the food was placed on the table for all to share Father Dimitros who was sat opposite Pharrell asked if he had had a fruitful day in the library.

"Yes, I believe I have had a good day and enjoyed the company of Father Antonio," Pharrell replied.

Father Antonio who was sat next to Father Dimitros looked at Pharrell and was wondering what Pharrell would say next. "Mr. Anderson, perhaps, we should leave business until we have finished searching the library."

"Have you found something that interests you Mr. Anderson?" Father Dimitros, interrupted.

"Yes, but I have not finished searching the library. When I have, I will be better able to answer your question, Father Dimitros," Pharrell replied.

"Mr. Anderson is on a quest, isn't true Mr. Anderson?" Father Antonio asked.

"Yes I am. My quest is to someday find the *Shahbla el Allah*."

Pharrell paused and gazed around the room at his fellow companions and saw that they were busy eating their goat broth and bread without engaging in conversation. Perhaps, the unfamiliar surroundings of a Christian monastery and priests were enough to quell their tongues. The age old rivalry between Christianity and Islam has lasted since the Crusades and he felt the same as though time had not healed the peace between these two religions. He had no faith in religion, especially, today, when religion was still being used as an excuse to slaughter innocents in the name of God.

"What are you thinking about, Mr. Anderson. You seem to be in contemplation about something," Father Dimitros asked.

Pharrell decided not reveal his thoughts, but instead to ask a question. "Have you heard the name Sheik Abul Adin?"

"No, I have not heard of this name before."

"Perhaps, you have heard of the 'Thief of Baghdad' a name associated with Sheik Abul Adin?" Pharrell asked.

"Yes, I have heard of this person, in fact, the whole of Egypt must have heard about the exploits of the 'Thief of Baghdad' who, apparently, stole most of the treasures stored in the national museum in Baghdad," Father Dimitros explained.

"You see Mr. Anderson even out here in the desert we read newspapers," Father Antonio interjected with a smile.

"Why do you ask?" Father Dimitros asked.

"I would like to find him and ask him about the *Shahbla el Allah*. Sometimes you have to dance with the devil to find what you want," Pharrell replied with a wry grin on his face.

"You do realise Mr. Anderson that the police and most of Egypt would like to know the whereabouts of this person. If you do find him then it's possible that you would become a wanted man as well."

"It's a chance I am willing to take; besides, I'm not willing to buy plundered artefacts from the 'Thief of Baghdad' just to find out what he knows about the *Shahbla el Allah* and that's it," Pharrell explained.

Pharrell noticed from the corner of his eye that Mohamed was listening to every word of his conversation. "Do you know where I perhaps will find him?"

"That's a dangerous question Mr. Anderson, and one even if I knew it would not be safe to answer," Father Dimitros replied.

Pharrell was puzzled by this answer and decided not to dwell on the answer. Perhaps, the company of his companions listening to every word would spook most Christians, especially, these priests out here in the wilderness.

"It's easy to find a cat amongst a pack of dogs. Perhaps, you need to look for the 'Thief of Baghdad' in the poorest district in Cairo where you will find plenty of thieves willing to take your money and there you will find the king of thieves willing to talk," Father Antonio exclaimed.

"Yes, you are probably right, Father Antonio. To catch a thief you need to walk among them," Pharrell said with a wry grin on his face.

That night outside the walls of the monastery Pharrell and Mohamed sat inside their tent talking as the other Arabs were fast asleep. It was the first time Pharrell felt wide awake and perhaps that was due to only a half a day abreast a camel. It was a hot night unusual for the desert and that was due to the clouds in the sky concealing the majestic beauty of the stars. Pharrell wondered if another desert storm was on its way.

"I noticed no stars tonight…perhaps this is a bad omen. What do you think, Mohamed?" Pharrell asked.

"There are many nights like tonight in the desert. It feels like a storm is coming, and, yet, it is hot and without the wind to cool the air. This could signal the coming of rain, we do have sudden rain storms, but, they are unusual, compared with sand storms that frequent these lands. I have noticed the climate changing year to year," Mohamed replied.

"You are not alone; Mohamed…the world is changing fast. The question is…are we hastening our own demise, only time will tell, but it could be too late," Pharrell said pausing briefly to look at Mohamed's reaction. "I believe we are at a tipping point."

"Do you mean climate change, Mr. Anderson?"

"Yes, climate change. You reach a certain point without being able to turn back the clock…the tipping point. I believe we are at that junction. Civilisations have come and gone in the past because of severe climate change and I have no reason to believe the future will be any different."

"Everything has an end…it's called the 'circle of life'," Mohamed said with a quiet tone of voice and pausing only to sip some wine Father Dimitros had given him. "From whence you came so shall ye return."

"But, we will not see it…it will be, perhaps, in a hundred years from now."

"You don't sound very optimistic about the future, Mr Anderson?"

"Yes, it sounds that way…but I do hope mankind finds a way to change."

"Man always wants more than he needs…this is the folly of man's existence," Mohamed replied.

Pharrell looked at Mohamed and realised that Mohamed was a thinker like him. There was more to Mohamed than he had previously thought. Perhaps,

Mohamed would know how to find the 'Thief of Baghdad' it was worth a try.

"You heard me ask Father Dimitros about the 'Thief of Baghdad'…what do you know?" Pharrell asked bluntly.

Mohamed paused for several minutes before answering. "Yes, I do know this man a buyer and seller of ancient relics of Egypt. The one they call the 'Thief of Baghdad' is well known in Egypt to the Bedouins. Whenever a Bedouin finds a relic of the past it usually ends up in the hands of the 'Thief of Baghdad' if it's valuable enough."

"Well then…how do I find him?" Pharrell asked impatiently.

"He will find you…if you have something of value to sell," Mohamed replied.

***

The following day Pharrell was busy searching through the library at the monastery with Father Antonio without success. There was only one book that made any commercial sense to Pharrell and that was one of the first books Father Antonio had shown him.

"Do you think Father Dimitros will sell the book on alchemy…the one you thought dated from the sixteenth century?" Pharrell asked.

"I don't know…you will have to ask him not me," Father Antonio replied.

***

Jac was at the Hilton hotel waiting in the reception area as instructed for Harry Lebervitz to arrive before making his way to the airport and catching the

afternoon flight to Cairo. As he sat there in a comfortable leather armchair he caught sight of Harry exiting the elevator holding a black briefcase. Jac briefly summarised that Harry was up to something, otherwise, why did he demand a nine o' clock meeting?
"Good morning, Jac," Harry said.
Harry was not his usual self, Jac thought, before replying," Good morning, Mr. Lebervitz.
Harry sat down opposite Jac and without a word opened his briefcase and handed Jac a brown envelope. Looking straight into Jac's eyes he said, "This is your bonus I promised you, plus, a bit more for your expenses in Egypt. I want you to find this 'Thief of Baghdad' as soon as possible. And don't forget to keep me informed on a daily basis."
"Oh, by the way, same as before no one is to be hurt, is that understood?"
"Of course, Mr. Levervitz,..as per your instructions."
Jac was thinking the opposite; sometimes you needed to shake a few people before they cooperated. It was sometimes a necessary evil. And one he had no qualms doing. He briefly remembered his last assignment when he had to cajole a previously uncooperative husband of a client, who at first refused to sign a divorce document, but after a few blows to the head the husband eventually signed the divorce document although reluctantly.
"What do I do, if I find this 'Thief of Baghdad' person?" Jac asked.
"Find what you can about him and more important find out if he deals in fakes and forgeries. And if he had anything to do with these papyri that I have just purchased from Hugo and Pharrell?"
"What about the Russian in Algeria?"
"Forget about him, he is just small fry."

"Anything else I should know?" Jac asked inquisitively hoping Harry would reveal more of his plans to him. But, none were forthcoming.

"No, just get on that plane. I expect a report from you later tonight."

***

The camel caravan was on its way to the city of Zafarana midway between Cairo and Luxor on the Nile River. The main highway followed the course of the meandering river straight to Cairo. That morning, Pharrell had made a deal with Father Dimitros for the book on alchemy, in exchange for the cost of supplies he had bought for the monastery plus an agreement of fifty percent of the eventual selling price. Pharrell was happy with this business agreement, at least, Father Dimitros trusted him to honour the agreement, he thought. As the caravan made its way through the sand dunes, and the monastery only visible in the distance when riding on top of a sand dune, Pharrell wondered as he last caught sight of the monastery, if the book on alchemy he had bought would be enough to tempt the 'Thief of Baghdad' from his hiding place.

"Well Jasmin, I hope I'm right," he said to himself and the camel.

The rain storm Mohamed had predicted had not yet materialised. But the wind was getting stronger by the hour. Only the occasional screech from a solitarily vulture high above in the sky could be heard above the sound of the whistling wind. Pharrell could see just blue sky and the lone vulture circling above, waiting for a free lunch as they trekked across the desert. Perhaps, Mohamed was wrong and another sand storm was due, he mused.

"No sign of rain," Pharrell said shouting ahead towards Mohamed who was leading the caravan.

Mohamed stopped and waited for Pharrell and his camel to come alongside him. "Be patient Mr. Anderson, it will come when least expected."

"It doesn't feel like rain. Normally, it rains when there are dark clouds in the sky. At the moment I see clear blue sky," Pharrell said.

"Yes, you are right. But, this is the desert, Mr. Anderson not Europe. Remember that we had two nights when the air was hot…that is unusual for most desert nights, and also, at the same time no wind to cool the air. This was a sign that rain is coming, believe me, the Bedouin know this land."

"But, you are not Bedouin, you told me, you were born in Aleppo, in Syria."

"Yes, what I told you are true, but my ancestors were Bedouin. The Bedouin Arabs go beyond borders, and have done this for thousands of years. In fact, you will find many Bedouin tribes are not Muslims either…and many practice no religion or faith. The only faith some Bedouin have, is the law on to them."

"What do you mean…the law on to them?" Pharrell asked curiously.

Mohamed paused momentarily and looked ahead of the caravan and then said, "Look ahead of the caravan and what do you see?"

Pharrell scanned the horizon for several minutes and then said, "I can only see sand dunes and the occasional scrubby bush."

"Yes, you are right. But, there is much you cannot see…that is, because you don't understand the ways of the Bedouin. The Bedouin Arabs have lived and died in the desert for thousands of years before the rise of Islam. The Bedouin respect nature and detest authority because they are a free people, and not aligned, to any particular country, religion or faith. And, that is how, it has been for the Bedouins for thousands of years," Mohamed explained.

"So, what can you see ahead," Pharrell asked.

"Look towards the horizon…do you see the dark clouds just above the horizon?" Mohamed replied.

"Yes, I do…but, only just."

"Well, there it is…the rain storm is approaching, most likely, within the next three to four hours just before sunset," Mohamed said calmly.

"The Bedouin are a law on to them…like the Americans, who believe they have all the answers," Pharrell remarked not expecting a reply to his jibe at the Americans.

As the caravan made its way from the mountain terrain onto the sand tunes, Pharrell often caught sight of distant mirages, and was often fooled, at first, into believing what he saw. He was sure in his mind that Angelique felt the same about him, as he did, about her. He could almost feel her body and occasionally imagine her scent almost like a mirage in the desert willing you to believe it's there, but, it's not there. You see what you want to see, instead of endless sand tunes; you see palm trees and a possible oasis. At least, the visit to the monastery had not been a complete waste of time, he now had some clues, and a possible way to tempt the 'Thief of Baghdad' out of his hiding place, he surmised.

"When do we reach Zafarana?" Pharrell asked.

"Around sunset, tomorrow, "Mohamed replied.

"The sun is starting to set and the clouds have turned black. And the coolness of the air chills my bones. When do we camp for the night?" Pharrell asked, as he felt the desert air against his face begin to chill his cheeks.

"Do you see that dry river bed up ahead," Mohamed said.

"Yes...," Pharrell replied, without thinking.

"Just beyond that river bed is a *Wadi*, where we can find some shelter for the night."

Indeed, when the rain did arrive, the rain poured like a water tap out of control and the dry river bed the caravan had been following was now like any other river in full torrid flow. A torrent of water was flowing in one direction towards its lowest point in the desert. Pharrell could see the sense in what Mohamed had said about taking shelter.

Pharrell noticed, the geology of the *wadi* walls offered protection from most of the wind like a valley in a mountain rage. Mohamed was right, the *wadi* indeed provided shelter from the wind, but, at least, the *wadi* was dry compared to the raging river nearby, he mused.

Pharrell noticed, how soon the day had turned to night, almost in an instant, the rain had eased to a constant drizzle when the caravan made camp for the night. The Arabs were quick to make fire, and he was glad to eat some hot food. The spices in the food warmed his blood, and he had decided to drink some hot camel's milk to help him sleep. Pharrell realised that Bedouin certainly knew how to keep alive in this desert.

"Tomorrow, I will arrange transport for you, to travel back to Cairo," Mohamed said, as he sat with Pharrell inside the tent. "You will be glad to get back to civilisation, and a soft bed. Is that, not true, Mr. Anderson?"

"You are right, Mohamed. A soft bed, yes...but civilisation, I'm not sure we as humans can be called civilised, when, most of the time humanity appears to want to destroy itself," Pharrell remarked.

"What district of Cairo would you suggest I start my search for the 'Thief of Baghdad,' when I get back to Cairo?"

"First, you will lucky to reach Cairo from Zafarana on the coast until very late in the evening, possible early the next day. So, it will be a couple of days before you can start your search for this man. And you will need to be careful…there are many criminals willing to take your money and kill for it," Mohamed exclaimed.

"Are you suggesting your services…are you willing to be my guide?" Pharrell asked.

"Yes, of course, Mr. Anderson. You will need someone who speaks the language and knows the country like I do. I'm happy to be your guide. We will start your search for the 'Thief of Baghdad' in the *Bab El Bahr* district of Cairo. The *Bab El Bahr* district is one of the poorest districts in Cairo. Most of the Arabs that live there are of Palestinian decent with a mix of refugees from other Arab countries that have found their way into Egypt over the years."

Pharrell needed to offer the book on alchemy as an item that would appeal to the greed of the Sheik's personality. It was said that the Sheik had his hands in most black market deals and also legitimate antiquity transactions. Pharrell's plan was simple, he planned to offer the book on alchemy bought from Father Dimitros for sale to several dealers in ancient artefacts around Cairo then it was more likely the black market dealers in artefacts would hear about it, and then possibly and hopefully the 'Thief of Baghdad' would surface and take the bait. Pharrell had been more than confident that this ruse would do the trick as he explained to

Mohamed; it would be like tricking a rabbit from its hole to surface so it could be caught.

"But, the real quest for you Mr. Anderson…is to find the *Shahbla el Allah* and not the 'Thief of Baghdad'. Perhaps, the lure you need…needs to be bigger than the fish you hope to catch?"

"What do you mean…the lure needs to be bigger than the fish you hope to catch?" Pharrell asked inquisitively trying to understand what Mohamed was proposing. He had a deep scowl now visible on his face questioning what he had just heard.

"It's like the lure of a beautiful woman…men are suddenly aroused. It's purely nature. So, we have to make the lure…something the 'Thief of Baghdad' cannot refuse."

Pharrell interrupting said, "What do you suggest?"

Mohamed paused to smile; it was the first time Pharrell had seen Mohamed smile. Pharrell had found Mohamed more of a mystery than the quest he was chasing. Mohamed appeared to be, at times, an unknown quantity, he thought.

***

As Pharrell and Mohamed walked the back streets of Cairo early the following morning, they had noticed there was an eerie quietness in the air before most Egyptians had reluctantly crawled out of their beds. Pharrell detected the faintest smell of a mix of petrol, food and incense from the previous night's endeavours in the air between the narrow streets and the slum buildings of the *Bab El Bahr* district of Cairo. Pharrell and Mohamed felt that it would be no surprise, if they found more than they bargained for in this hell hole.

"I'm glad you are watching my back, Mohamed. Because, this place doesn't feel friendly, and usually I trust my intuition to be right," Pharrell exclaimed.

"No, you are right, Mr. Anderson. This place is full of thieves willing to take your money at every street you cross. Luckily, you have me to guide and protect you."

"I feel, so many eyes are watching every move I make, whereas, you blend into the background." Pharrell said, while suggesting with his hand towards, Mohamed. "Inside that Café earlier, most eyes were on me and not you."

"A foreigner in a foreign land sticks out like a cat amongst a pack of dogs," Pharrell explained.

"You are right, Mr. Anderson, especially, when you are walking the streets in a poor area," Mohamed said.

"The rent is cheap, but with many prying eyes," the Arab seller said.

"We were told you buy and sell ancient artefacts…is that the case. My name is Pharrell Anderson, and this is my friend, Mohamed. We have something to sell," Pharrell said, while surveying the scene. At first sight, most of the space was taken with an array of antique repro furniture carefully laid out amongst the genuine artefacts. Some of the statues probably had dubious provenance, Pharrell was thinking. Making money in this country from grave robbing and other activities, was just like they did when their ancestors were building the great pyramids the thieves were already ready and waiting to plunder your grave as soon as someone died.

It was shades of grey if you avoided the dust and dirt and dug deep to find your treasures, Pharrell mused, as he spoke with the Arab seller.

"What can I do for you, sir?" the Arab seller asked.

"What do you have for sale…on the black market?" Pharrell asked smiling openly with the cheek of a child wanting another sweet. "What can you offer me…?" Mohamed looked on, in disgust, at such a direct question to ask.

The Arab seller asked interrupting abruptly, "What do really want, sir?"

"To meet the 'Thief of Baghdad' his real name is Sheik Abul Adin."

The Arab seller looked straight into Pharrell's eyes before jesting to Pharrell that most of Egypt would like know the whereabouts of the infamous 'Thief of Baghdad' the antiquities dealer. The police and the government had been unsuccessful in their attempts to catch the Sheik. Even though the local and national newspapers in Egypt had repeatedly published articles and pictures of the Sheik, nobody knew or was willing to say where the Sheik was hiding. There were many rumours over the years that the Sheik had taken flight and was probably living in another country. There were rumours that the Sheik had friends in prominent positions in the Egyptian government, because they were sympathetic to the Sheik's Palestinian cause.

"If you want to see the Sheik than at first, you must give him a reason to see you."

"Tell him…I have a book of prophecies dated sixteenth century to offer him, in exchange, for the knowledge he has for the *Shahbla el Allah*," Pharrell said with authority knowing how to lure a big fish in a small pond. At first, offer the bait and attempt to lure the big fish from the shadows. Hopefully, the 'Thief of Baghdad' will surface in a day or two, he was sure.

***

The following day Pharrell and Mohamed, had decided to visit the national museum in Cairo and they were unaware they were being followed.

"Do you think the Sheik will see me?" Pharrell asked.

"You have to be patient, sir. Don't forget there is perhaps a long line of intermediaries before the message gets to the top dog," Mohamed replied.

"Mohamed, you have a way with words. I don't imagine the Sheik would like to be referred to as a top dog."

"You see this cartouche of Hatshepsut, the hieroglyphics of this monument show how the ancient Egyptian Pharaohs were idolised as Gods, in the form, of a living God. To the people their Pharaohs were the living intermediaries between their many Gods and themselves." Mohamed quickly looked around the main room exhibiting many large and impressive statues of long ago Gods.

"Today, it's the government and its agencies that control the people…and not their Gods and Pharaohs, "Mohamed said pausing only to scan the room before continuing his conversation with Pharrell. "Today, there are many, so-called top dogs running the country."

"What have you seen?" Pharrell asked inquisitively.

"I think we are being followed," Mohamed replied in a whisper.

That's not unusual, Pharrell thought, "I felt like all eyes were watching us, yesterday, in that slum district."

"You are right, sir, but that was expected, because we looked like a couple of wealthy tourists lost in a poor district of Cairo. Today, we are like any other tourist visiting their national museum, in the right place. We don't look out of place like a fish out of water."

"Are you sure, we are being followed?" Pharrell asked as he carefully made a mental note himself of the faces of the people in the museum. He was trying to look one way when he caught sight of Harry Lebervitz's man. The same man that had followed him and Hugo around France for weeks, he only had a quick glimpse of him, but he was sure it was Harry Lebervitz's man.

"Not to worry, Mohamed," Pharrell said.

"I'm not worried, sir, but, it's safer to know and not know you are being followed," Mohamed retorted.

As Pharrell and Mohamed stood outside the museum they caught sight of a melee of tourists trying to queue while Arabs tried to sell them everything from watches to priceless antiques that looked too good to be genuine.

"Please, sir, take my taxi...if you want the '*Shahbla el Allah*'," the Arab taxi driver said in a whisper of a voice.

Pharrell and Mohamed at first were shocked at these words, but suddenly, realised, this was it, a chance to see the infamous 'Thief of Baghdad' finally after countless days searching for him. They got into the taxi with trepidation and not expecting what happened next as the taxi sped away across the city of Cairo. The taxi eventually stopped and two Arabs got in and demanded Pharrell and Mohamed where hoods before the taxi sped off again.

"Don't be afraid Mr. Anderson...the hood is for our protection...you are not being kidnapped. We will take you to see the 'Thief of Baghdad' our boss."

Inside the hood Pharrell could easily hear what was being said, but not sure from whom. It was too hot at the best of times in Egypt, but inside a black hood the heat was like in a sauna, sweat was already steadily pouring down his face, he felt the sweat trickling down his forehead and onto his neck as the taxi car twisted and turned its way around the streets of Cairo. I hope this turns out for the best, he whispered to himself.

"Mohamed, do not worry, this is for your protection, we are nearly there...the 'Thief of Baghdad' awaits your arrival," said a voice inside the second car.

"You and your friend Pharrell Anderson are safe," said the voice of another man. This time the taxi car stopped and Mohamed was helped into another car before he could sense he was on his own. "Where are you taking me," Mohamed asked with his voice being muffled by the hood over his head.

"Don't worry we are nearly there," an Arab sounding voice replied.

Pharrell was unaware his friend Mohamed was in a different part of the city. The first time the taxi had stopped was when the switch had been made. They told Pharrell that Mohamed was in another room, and was not needed because the Sheik spoke perfect English.

As Pharrell's hood was removed, even the light of a poorly lit room, at first, blinded his vision; he's eyes needing several seconds before he could successfully scan the room. The room had no windows and there was only an old beaten up desk and two high back wooden chairs in the centre of the room. The walls and ceiling had seen better days with a mismatch of colors and some graffiti on the plaster, but Pharrell could not read the Arabic lettering.

"Sorry, to have you hooded, it's for your protection, now, what is it that you want from me? I am the 'Thief of Baghdad' the man you have been trying to find."

"You are Sheik Abul Adin, I am Pharrell Anderson, I am honoured to meet you...you have quite a reputation," Pharrell said offering his hand.

"I'm a businessman, in to make money not to lose it, so, what have you got to offer me?" the Sheik's voice roared as he leaned back in his chair.

"Tell me what you know about the *Shahbla el Allah*, and, in exchange I will offer you a book of prophecies dated early sixteenth century." Pharrell exclaimed hoping the man knew more than he did, and that his lure would loosen his tongue sufficiently worth the value of the antiquarian book.

"First! Please, take a seat, and have some refreshments. You must be thirsty after your journey here," the Sheik exclaimed.

Pharrell took advantage of the refreshments and eagerly awaited the Sheik's information.

"You have to understand that many adventurers like yourself would like to find the treasure chest, in your case, the *Shahbla el Allah*, why do you think, if I knew, where to find it that I would tell you. You are misplaced in your assessment of me, Mr Anderson."

"I think you…"

Pharrell said, interrupting the Sheik "Wait, before you answer. I understand this. I just want to know, what you know, about the legend of the '*Shahbla el Allah*' and that's it. It's a straightforward deal. You tell me everything you know and I will offer the book in exchange. It's a fair offer. I hope you can see this."

"You sound like a man I can trust, Mr. Anderson."

The Sheik shouted out some order in Arabic and a servant arrived through the only door into the room carrying two *Hookers* already burning a pleasant smelling substance as the smoke filled the room. The servant placed them on the desk next to the coffee.

"Okay, we have a deal Mr. Anderson," the Sheik replied as he gestured with his hands, to take the smoking *hooker* from the servant. A few more words from the Sheik in Arabic and the servant scurried away. The '*Shahbla el Allah*' has been a legend for centuries, and, will probably never be found, because it's difficult to find the unexpected when it's expected," the Sheik said.

The Sheik momentarily paused, and then said, "Do you understand what I have just said, Mr. Anderson?"

Pharrell said, "I'm not sure…please explain what you mean, *it's difficult to find the unexpected when it's expected*? What does that mean?"

"It's similar to the phrase: a poison chalice, but, you expect to find the '*Shahbla el Allah*' and then when you do not…this is when, you are likely to overlook the chance of finding the treasure," the Sheik explained.

"Please, go on," Pharrell said encouragingly.

The Sheik paused, and took several puffs from the hooker's sweet smelling smoke, and then said, "Mr. Anderson, you must understand that the legend of the '*Shahbla el Allah*' comes from the Babylonians whom occupied a region of what is now called Iraq around one thousand years before Christ. You also must realise that the word *Shahbla* is an ancient Aramaic word used to describe a story and that the word *Shahbla* in a modern text is used loosely to mean a book. But, the word *Shahbla* in the Kurdish region of Iraq means something else. The Yazidis, who have lived in the region for thousands of years, and are most likely, the living ancestors of the Babylonians, and they use this word *Shahbla* or something very close to mean: an opening. Literally, meaning to open, or an opening. There is much you should learn about the culture and language of the Yazidis, because these tribes are the true descendants of the ancient Babylonians."

"There is much to learn, I can see what you are trying to say," Pharrell said, as he tried to inhale the sweet smoke from the *Hooker* pipe, before encouraging the Sheik to go on with his hands.

"Do you understand, Mr. Anderson?"

"Yes, I believe I do."

"*It's difficult to find the unexpected when it's expected*" the Sheik said again, only pausing to see the reaction from Pharrell, who felt under pressure from the questioning, it was not what he had expected from the Sheik.

"Listen, you tell me everything you know about the 'Shahbla el Allah' that was the deal…I didn't expect a school lesson," Pharrell said abruptly.

"Mr. Anderson you have to have patience. If I knew where to find the *Shahbla el Allah* then I would have found it by now. Whoever told you that I would know where to find it was mistaken. Everyone calls me the 'Thief of Bagdad' without understanding who I am. The police, the government, and the newspapers like to think they know me, but, there is much they do not know. Like the shifting sand dunes in a desert I cannot stay too long in one place before I must move on."

"Is that it?" demanded Pharrell.

"What did you expect? I gave you what I know. It's up to you how you interpret this information and what you do next. I didn't think I could refuse your offer. It was so generous an offer…to refuse. It's now up to you to honour that offer," the Sheik replied.

"Of course, I will honour our bargain. Before, I give you the book on alchemy and prophecies I would like to know your appraisal on the book's value, so I can reimburse my partner their share of the book's value."

"Did you know that Abu the street thief in the 'Thief of Baghdad' was born in Iraq? And, is from a story from the 'Arabian Night's?" the Sheik asked.

"No, I didn't know that the 'Thief' was born in Iraq, but, I'm familiar with the story in the Arabian Nights," Pharrell replied.

"The book on alchemy is worth what it's worth; it's up to you to resolve the compensation you owe your partner, and not me. It was a street thief that helped a prince regains his crown from the usurper that ruled the land in this time in Baghdad. How Abu unlocks the secrets along his adventure with the prince are the real treasures, but often overlooked by the readers of the 'Arabian Nights' storyline."

"What do you mean?" Pharrell asked eagerly he wanted to learn these so called secrets.

"I do not have the time to revisit the 'Arabian Nights' and tell you the story of the 'Thief of Baghdad,' so, you will have to read it if you want to know the secrets contained in the storyline. It's the most likely the only way you will learn the secrets, if you care to take the time to read the story again."

"Yes, but, how does this relate to my quest?" Pharrell asked grasping at clues, trying to tease out an answer from the Sheik.

"Our business is complete...you have some more information. And, I have to fade into the shadows again. My associates will blindfold you again and return you to your hotel...expect a changeover in the cars back to your hotel. Enjoy, your evening meal, and it's been a pleasure to meet you Mr. Anderson."

It was dark again inside the hood as Pharrell sat in the back of the car travelling towards the centre of Cairo. What secrets did the Sheik mean were the words he said to himself, as the car stopped, and he was pushed into another vehicle? One thing was certain, the Sheik, had made him eager to learn the secrets that lay hidden in the story of Abu the 'Thief of Baghdad' in the 'Arabian Knights', as soon as possible.

***

"It's me, Jac. Is that you Mr. Lebervitz?"
"Yes, go ahead…what news do you have, tonight?" Lebervitz asked.
"I have seen Pharrell Anderson, and he has been looking for the 'Thief of Bagdad' the same man you asked me to investigate. Apparently, on the street, the information is, he would like to meet the 'Thief'.
"Do you know why Anderson wants to meet with the Sheik?" Lebervitz asked.
"No, but I'm working on it," Jac replied.
"What else do you know about our target?"
"The Sheik is the main man in Egypt, and when it comes to buying and selling legal and black market antiquities, especially, when the price is right."
"Does he sell fakes and forgeries?" Lebervitz asked nervously not wanting to hear a positive answer.
"No, as far as I can tell…the Sheik is too busy buying and selling genuine artefacts. He often does business with clients through intermediaries, and, is seen as, good for the money. That's it."
"Okay, fine…keep me informed. See what else you can find out." Lebervitz said as the only sound Jac heard next was the phone line disconnecting. Typically Harry Lebervitz at his best, he never asked where I saw Pharrell Anderson, too ahead of himself to be bothered to ask, perhaps, this information could be used to make some extra money at a later date.

***

The professor was probably right about her guess that a 'grave digger' the most likely to find the *Shahbla,* before he did, thought Pharrell. "Hey, Joachim, How's it going there? The phone connection is a bit crackly, you'll have to speak louder, and otherwise I can't here you."

"Okay, here, had a rush on those 'double o seven' books, since the recent hype on the next 'Bond' movie. And the weather here is shit, we have had so much snow for the last few days that the roads have been a nightmare to contend with. Otherwise, business is good," Joachim replied.

"Find out what you can on the 'Yazidis of Iraq...their history and religion in the past and the present. Somewhere and somehow...there are clues hidden in the information you find out."

"What do you mean clues?" Joachim asked.

"Just find out what you can about the Yazidis, I believe there are clues, perhaps a reason why a traded a reasonably valuable book for this information."

"Okay, boss...will do," Joachim replied.

"Yes, I traded the book on alchemy, that I bought from Father Dimitros at the monastery in the middle of the desert, valued around ten thousand dollars for the information the Sheik Abul Adin also known as the 'Thief of Baghdad' gave me," Pharrell said.

"You sound like, you are not sure about what you bought, Pharrell?"

"No, it was something the Sheik said, he said, because *it's difficult to find the unexpected when it's expected.* He was referring to my quest to find the '*Shahbla el Allah*' and since then...sat here, on the bed in my hotel room...I have had to think about my quest, how, I feel about Angelique and where to go from here. It seems like destiny has given me a crossroads to make a decision about which road I take. Plus, the sweat is pouring from me…there seems no let-up in the heatwave Cairo is experiencing right now."

"Okay, though it's better to be too hot than shivering your nuts to pieces. You need to upgrade the heating in this rat hole," Joachim said.

"You could be right, Joachim, but, for now just find out what you can." Pharrell could feel more sweat trickle down the side of his face onto his wet shirt. The heat was unbearable at times, but, if you had a choice and his would be to be hot, and not shivering your balls off, where you cannot feel your fingers or your toes. But, Joachim was right the whole shop needed new heating. Perhaps, now, would be a good time to think about his relationship with Angelique. His body warmed at the thought of her. Every day his love of Angelique had grown stronger. His thoughts were often more about how he felt about Angelique and, not about his quest that he had, if he was honest with himself, it had become an obsession. The quest to find the '*Shahbla el Allah*' had become both an obsession and a curse. And, he had seen how his friend Hugo had reacted during their recent business together. Pharrell realised that greed at some point, it would seem, knocks on your door and many can be easily tempted.

***

Angelique was busy watching the road; her thoughts were with the mission. But, at the end of the mission, she had other ideas. In the meantime, the Thai mafia were on the move.

"It looks like the cargo…is on the move," Angelique said.
"Let me know when it arrives at its destination," the section head said. The secure phone line disconnected. In the meantime, Angelique kept a safe distance as she followed the truck in her car. She had already arranged for another agent to take over the surveillance at *Nakhon Pathom*, believing the truck was heading for somewhere near Bangkok.

***

"What will you do know?" Mohamed asked, curiously wanting to know if his employment with Anderson had finally finished its journey.
Pharrell replied, "I thank you, for your help. Tonight, I will have some drinks from the hotel bar, and think about my next move. You are welcome to join me. Tomorrow is another day."
"Yes, you are right. It is time to think. And, I will join you Mr. Anderson," Mohamed said pausing only briefly to collect his thoughts before continuing. "Have you had a profitable time here…in Egypt?"
Pharrell had got used to Mohamed's direct questions and paused momentarily before answering, "Time will tell…at the moment…I feel like I have more questions that need answers. And what does…*it's difficult to find the unexpected when it's expected*…mean?"
Mohamed sipped the wine he had recommended and paused curling his lips in anticipation of the gratification of revealing a possible reply to Mr. Anderson. Mohamed thought, Pharrell appeared cagey in his replies, yet wanting honest opinions. "The Sheik has given you a riddle. The Arabs are famous in these desert lands for riddles."

"What do you mean a riddle?" Pharrell demanded.

"A riddle...a riddle...a set of words with a hidden meaning," Mohamed explained.

"And what does... *it's difficult to find the unexpected when it's expected*...mean in this riddle?" Pharrell asked hoping for an answer.

"The answer could mean many things. The Arabs have a different culture, and a different way of thinking, so, my answer will not be your way of thinking. For example: If you are mining for gold, you will perhaps overlook the silver deposits and other valuable deposits because you are looking for what you are expecting. Perhaps this analogy of the riddle is wrong. It is how you see this riddle; it is then that you will be able to decipher its true meaning."

"Now, I can see what you are trying to say."

"A riddle is for you to answer; only you can really understand what the Sheik was trying to say to you, Mr. Anderson. The riddle is there to guide your path. The Sheik gave you more than you were expecting, or indeed expected."

"Perhaps, you are right. I just don't know it, yet, Mohamed."

"Are you closer to your quest now than before you came to Egypt? " Mohamed enquired.

"I said before...I have more questions than answers, and my quest seems more elusive than before because I think I know more than I did before. And that is a riddle," Pharrell said with a broad smile, as Mohamed caught the glimpse of a smile often seen from a purring cat.

"Tell me...what you know about the 'Yazidis?' Pharrell asked calmly while supping his wine.

"Why do you ask Mr. Anderson?" Mohamed asked.

"First, tell me what you know about the Yazidis? Then I will tell you why," Pharrell asked, with a wry smile brimming across his face turning a reddish blush from the alcohol, he had drank.

"They are people that inhabit parts of Iraq, just like the Kurds who are non-Muslim, although some perhaps do practice Islam. But, most of the Yazidis practice their own religion, which like I said, is non-Muslim."

Mohamed explained that the Yazidis are a tribe of Arabs that have lived in Iraq for thousands of years; some say they are the founders of the land of Iraq. Before, the western powers decided to carve up the Middle East the Yazidis lived largely in the northern part of Iraq and today the Yazidis are separated by borders, across a range of countries, such as Turkey, Syria, and Iraq.

"Are you a Yazidis?" Pharrell asked inquisitively.

"No, but you are close. I am an Arab Bedouin. But, I am from the same part of Iraq and I know many Yazidis. And I have many friends that are Yazidis. Then again, I have many friends from many countries."

"Continue…Mohamed. And tell me more about the Yazidis?"

Suddenly, a waiter approached their table. "Would you like another drink?" the waiter asked.

Pharrell ordered another round of drinks for them both, before urging Mohamed to continue talking about the Yazidis. For some reason, the 'Thief of Baghdad' had told him the Yazidis was the key to finding the '*Shahbla*' and somehow and somewhere he had to find the clue, he mused.

"Please, continue…Mohamed. And tell me more about the Yazidis?"

"They are monotheists, and they believe in one God, just like the Jews and many other faiths, yet, today, they have been persecuted by Islamic fundamentalists for being Arab and non-Muslim," Mohamed said.

Pharrell interrupted, "That's the problem when fanatics take over, especially, when religion controls our minds rather than logic."

"Yes, you are right Mr. Anderson. Religion in the past has been responsible for many wars and I see no different for the future. The Yazidis are treated by the Iraq government as a separate ethnic group; as a minority like the Christians in an Arab country with many religionist fanatics with no will for peace."

"When the Americans and others invaded Iraq during the Gulf War and deposed of Saddam Hussein from power they unleased a can of worms," Pharrell interjected with wry smile on his face.

"Today, it's not safe in some areas to highlight your faith. The Yazidis are mainly Kurdish speaking but some speak Arabic. The history of the Yazidis is largely obscure, with little or no scholarly work done to find out the history of this tribe. Some scholars suggest that the Yazidis are the descendants of the ancient Babylonians. That much is known and much else little known...the Yazidis are one of least understood tribes in present times. There you are...that is all I know about the Yazidis, now you can tell me why you want to know about them?" Mohamed asked.

"It was something the Sheik said to me, when he asked me about my quest," Pharrell replied.

"Why do you think the Sheik wanted you to find out about the Yazidis? Mohamed asked.

"At the moment, I don't know why?" Pharrell proclaimed innocently.

"Perhaps, you need to go back to the beginning. From the beginning, you can retrace your steps and possibly find the clue you are looking for. Sometimes, it's easier to find the answer when you are not looking for it," Mohamed said calmly.

"Tomorrow, I will book a flight back to Bangkok and see my girlfriend, and from there fly back to Norway. The summer season for me is nearly over and I need to consider my plans for the future. My quest will have to wait, I guess, until I have finalised my plans for the future," Pharrell said dejectedly.

"You sound defeated, sir," Mohamed said.

"Do I...Mohamed."

"Yes. Yet, you have had an adventure and perhaps someday you will appreciate this. You tell me that you have found the woman of your dreams. Yet, you are not satisfied. This is the problem that affects man. Men never know when the well is full and therefore are never satisfied. The Arabs have a saying – the circle is never complete."

"There you go, Mohamed...with your way with words."

"But, it is true, sir."

"Have you heard the story about the richest man in Babylon?" Mohamed asked.

"No. I don't believe I have. I guess, you are about to tell me...is that true?" Pharrell asked.

"No, I will not tell you the story...because it would take too long for me to tell you the whole story now. Besides, you will enjoy finding the story and reading it for yourself. I will only tell you that many people who have read this story fail to find the real meaning of the story. People rush to read the story, but fail to find the true meaning or moral of the story. But, because we are friends, I will tell you the secret hidden within the story. It is simple. *Don't overlook the opportunities that life presents to you.* That is it," Mohamed replied.

"Thanks, I will read the story and when I do, I will think of you. You have been a good friend to me these past days," Pharrell said sincerely, as he took a large gulp of liquor before continuing. "What will you do when I go?"

"The same as before I met you…just ferrying tourists and adventurers through the desert on the back of a camel, and, occasionally around Cairo, and other parts of Egypt. Its simple work, but one I enjoy," Mohamed replied.

"I think I need another drink to help me sleep tonight, although some of that camel's milk did the trick before. Would you like another drink, Mohamed?" Pharrell asked.

"No, I have had enough. Besides, it's getting late and I must go. I have friends to visit in Cairo before I return to my Bedouin brothers."

"Thanks, for all your help."

"You are welcome, sir."

As Mohamed stood up from the table to leave, Pharrell caught sight of Harry Lebervitz's man, it was the same man he had seen at the Cairo museum and in Paris he was sure. He was sitting at a table partially obscured by the hotel's bar. Perhaps, it was time he introduced himself, he said to himself.

***

"Hello, it's Jac."

"Hello, its Harry Lebervitz here, tell me what news you have for me."

"You asked me to find out why Pharrell Anderson wanted to find the 'Thief of Baghdad' also known as Sheik Abul Adin. Well, it seems that Anderson was told that the Sheik held information about the '*Shahbla el Allah*' a book about God. Apparently, Anderson and the Sheik met at an undisclosed place somewhere in Cairo, earlier today. I followed Anderson and his companion from the Cairo museum, but…"

Harry interrupted, "Who was the companion?"

"I'm not sure, an Arab…possibly, someone hired to translate for Anderson."

"Find out what you can about this Arab?"

"Shall I continue, Mr Lebervitz?" Jac replied sarcastically.

"Yes, of course." Harry snapped back.

Jac could hear the frustration in Harry's voice, and for once was glad. He was getting impatient with Harry's manner even though Harry Lebervitz was paying the bills.

"Like I said, I was following them around the Cairo museum and when they took a taxi from there, I followed the taxi for some distance until I lost them in the back streets of Cairo."

"Wait, how do you know Anderson met with the Sheik, earlier today?" Harry asked intently.

"I was wondering when you were going to ask me that."

"Never mind that, answer the question," Harry asked again.

"Earlier tonight, while I was observing Anderson and his Arab companion in their hotel in the lounge bar, and just as the Arab got up from their table to leave Anderson approached my table and he introduced himself to me. Just as I said before in Paris, he knew my face and he knows that I'm working for you."

"What did Anderson have to say?" Harry asked inquisitively.

"He asked why I was following him."

"Did you tell him?"

"I didn't have to, he had already guessed and told me," Jac replied.

"So, what did you talk about?"

"Anderson told me that he met with the Sheik and exchanged a valuable book on alchemy for information on the '*Shahbla el Allah*' and that he was planning to fly back to Norway the following day."

"Is that it?" Harry asked.

"Yes, more or less that's it."

"Are you sure, he didn't say anything more," Harry persisted in his questioning.

"He wanted to know why I was following him. So, I told him what he already knew, nothing more," Jac replied.

"Good," Harry said.

"What do you want me to do know?"

Momentarily, there was a break in the conversation as Harry thought for few seconds before replying to Jac's question. "Find out what you can on this Arab and find out what he knows about Anderson," Harry replied.

"Okay, and will you send me some more money for expenses?" Jac asked as he heard the sound of a grunt before the phone line went dead. Typically, Harry Lebervitz, he said to himself.

***

Pharrell used his time on the flight back to Bangkok to compile a list of the facts he had on the '*Shahbla el Allah*' and compare the list of information Henri and Cherie Piccar had given him in Paris. He was looking for clues. Perhaps, Hugo would know what to do next. He had come to a dead end. Pharrell was sure there had to be more, there was something he was missing, and he was sure, but what?

On a piece of paper he had begun to list the facts he had. He drew a line down the middle of the paper and on the left side listed all the facts he had on the *Shahbla* and on the right side listed all facts and information he had received from Henri and Cherie Piccar. One piece of information stood out like a sore thumb.

As soon as the plane landed Pharrell was busy trying to contact Angelique from the airport, but there was no answer from the telephone number she had given him before they parted. Instead he decided to call his friend, Hugo.

"Hello, Hugo is that you?" Pharrell asked.

"Yes, it's me, is that you Pharrell?"

"Where are you at the moment?" Pharrell asked intently.

"I'm in Bangkok, trying to be inconspicuous. Oh, by the way, I have a message for you from Angelique. It seems she has gone back to America. Apparently, her editor wanted to see her about covering another story. She phoned me to tell you to contact the receptionist at the offices of the magazine she works for."

"Did she say anything else?" Pharrell asked keenly.

"No, that was it. You are to contact her where she works. That was the message."

"Okay, will do. In the meantime, can we meet up in Bangkok later today? I have some information to discuss and some questions to ask you, is that okay with you?"

"Sure, *mon ami*. Where do you suggest?" Hugo asked.

"I'm in a taxi on my way to the hotel now. The same hotel I stayed at before, the Grand Hotel on *Soi* six, near the metro station."

"Yes, I know. Let's say in a couple of hours. Would that be okay?"

"Yes, that's fine. As long as this taxi driver can get through the traffic in time," Pharrell replied while observing the gridlock of vehicles trying to meander through the midday Bangkok traffic jam.

"Okay, see you later, *mon cher ami*."

Pharrell's taxi ride to the Grand Hotel from the airport was slow and tedious. He observed that the traffic lights in Bangkok lasted longer on red then they did in Norway. He needed a shower and a drink. He felt the sweat trickle down his back, and the heat of the city centre combined with the pollution from the traffic had started to choke his throat. In the meantime, his mobile was ringing, it was Joachim.

"Hello, Joachim."

"Hello, Boss."

"Call me Pharrell, you should know that?"

"I do, but sometimes, I can't help myself. Anyway, I have some information about the Yazidis people. Apparently, the Yazidis as a tribe date back, some believe, that is, some archaeologists to around the first and second century before Christ. "

"Much of this I already know."

Joachim said, "They seem to be a mysterious people, not much is known about the Yazidis there has been little or no research into their past. They're one of the only tribes that are truly mysterious in our modern times. The only thing that stands out is their religion."

"What did you say?"

"Oh, yes, their religion…that was it. Apparently, some archaeologists, who have studied their religion, suggest it goes back before the Torah and the Bible."

"Perhaps, the Sheik was right; when he said a clue, definitely, he would follow the Yazidis?" The truth had been hiding waiting to be discovered, Pharrell said to himself.

"And, that riddle, you mentioned before. Well, I have been thinking about that as well."

"You have been creative." Pharrell replied rhetorically.

"I think it really means: don't expect to find what you're looking for because if it were easy then someone else would have already found it. Does that make sense?"

"If it makes sense to you…then that's all that matters." Pharrell replied rudely before continuing to speak his thoughts. "I think it's what you said about their religion is the key and the riddle is just a red herring there to confuse the actors and the players in this game."

"What do you mean, boss…I mean Pharrell?"

"The sheik is a businessman; he isn't going to give all he knows for ten thousand dollars for something that could be worth hundreds of thousands of dollars, perhaps millions. The Yazidis are a race of people that are, perhaps, connected with the *Shahbla* somehow and then there is the riddle both could be red herrings, who knows. But, I found the sheik to be honest in his business dealings. So, I have no reason to believe he sold me dud information."

"So, where do we go from here?" Joachim asked keenly.

"Well, find out what you can on their religion – everything and anything, and their beliefs, what makes them so mysterious. I'm planning to return to Norway in a few days' time, in the meantime, find out what you can as fast as you can, *pronto*. And, let me know as soon as possible, day or night."

***

"Hello, can I speak with Angelique Bergerhof?" Pharrell asked calmly.

"She is out of the office at the moment. Can I take a message?" the voice asked.

"Yes, can you tell Angelique that Pharrell Anderson phoned and would she please contact him at the Grand Hotel in Bangkok room 198 on this telephone number. Pharrell then carefully repeated the telephone number twice to the receptionist. "Please, can you tell Angelique that it is the same hotel I stayed at before, she will understand. Thank you."

"Yes, of course. Is there anything else, I can help you with?" the receptionist asked.

"No, just please get this message to Angelique and goodbye," Pharrell replied.

As Pharrell finished dressing after a welcome shower the hotel's bedroom telephone rang and he rushed to answer it, hoping it was Angelique.

"Hello, sir, there is a Hugo Deschamps in reception to see you," the receptionist said trying her best to speak English.

"Okay, tell him, I will be right down and I will see him in the hotel bar," Pharrell replied, but momentarily deflated, hoping the telephone call would have been from Angelique and not from his friend. In his haste to get to the hotel's bar he noticed his reflection in the steel door of the elevator on the way down, he had forgotten to comb his hair; it looked like a tangled mop. Pharrell quickly scanned the hotel's bar and was satisfied he wasn't being watched. He had time to notice the commotion as a bus load of guests were returning from their day trip and watched as some of them were wearily making their way to the hotel's bar. He then caught sight of his friend sat at a table by a window with a view of the main entrance to the hotel.

"Hello, my good friend."

"*Mon cher ami*, you look like that desert sand wore you down?" Hugo remarked with a grin on his face as large as life. "You wanted to see me? How can I help?"

"I need your advice and knowledge"

"*Mon cher ami*, tell me what you want to know?"

"Well, first, there are these people called the Yazidis, that according to Sheik Abul Adin also known as the 'Thief of Baghdad' told me that I should study. Then there is this riddle."

"Riddle, what riddle?"

"A riddle the Sheik told me: it goes like this: *it's difficult to find the unexpected when it's expected*."

"And, there is more, but first I need a drink." Pharrell quickly caught the eye of the waiter and ordered a round of drinks before continuing. "What do you think, Hugo?"

"Well, first you haven't really told me anything of substance. A riddle and something about the Yazidis people isn't much to digest and form an opinion. The riddle – how does it go again?" Pharrell slowly repeated the riddle to Hugo while Hugo then repeated word for word the riddle to himself.

"Okay, *'it's difficult to find the unexpected when it's expected'* is clever and also frustrating at the same time. Hugo looked at Pharrell with a smile and said, "The riddle is the easy part. The information about the Yazidis will take a lot more analysis before I can comment on that."

"Would you like anything else," the waiter said, as he placed the drinks on their table. Pharrell paid and tipped the waiter generously and judging by the beaming smile on the waiter's face he was well pleased, and would be eager, no doubt, to serve their table again in a hurry, Pharrell said to himself.

"What do you mean the riddle is easy?"

"Perhaps, after another drink or two, you will see the answer as I do?"

"Don't jest with me, Hugo. Please tell me. I'm tired and I value your advice and experience."

"Well, okay. The riddle is similar to the law of chance; remember I spoke about the law of favourability when we went with Lucy to the casino in Paris. This is another one of those laws of the universe that are spread across time. By chance someone finds something and so they find the unexpected when least expected. Do you see, Pharrell?"

"What about the Yazidis?"

"*Mon ami*, I told you before you need to tell me more about them before I can tell you what I think?"

"They live in an area which is now part of Turkey, Syria and Iraq. The tribe or race is non-Muslim, who see themselves as Arabs, but do not follow Islam. Their religion is monotheistic, they believe in one God and that's about all I know?"

"Now, that you have told me more – you have refreshed my memory."

"Yes, two years ago, I was on a trail similar to your quest – looking for lost history when I came across, or should I say I was introduced to a man, an old man, with a beard as unkempt as mine and he had more grey hair on his head then me. A diminutive figure, I remember, but an imposing one. He told me his name, but I can't remember his name right now, although his name is on the tip of my tongue, only, that he was from northern Iraq and he was a Yazidis. I remember asking him about the Yazidis culture."

Hugo explained to Pharrell what the old man had said to him about the Yazidis. He explained that the Yazidis were an ancient tribe that originate from the collapse and destruction of Babylon around the first and second centuries before Christ. The old man described how the ancient Babylonians had been masters of their own demise. The legend, he explained, in the Bible had prophesised this before it happened.

"What happened?" Pharrell said eagerly with both hands clasped around his glass eager to know more before he needed another drink.

"*Mon cher ami*, have patience," Hugo replied with a wide grin on his face. "Remember, that patience is a virtue."

Hugo continued to explain what the old man had told him. The old man explained how Babylon had courted its own disaster. Soon after, the Jews were freed from their captivity in Babylon; it was then that he said Babylon started to crumble. It was not an earthquake that created the demise of Babylon, but the decimation of the population. When the Jews were set free – all the skills they had went back to Israel. The old man went on to say that the Jews that stayed he believed eventually became the Yazidis people. Hugo explained that the old man stressed that he believed the Yazidis were a mixture of old Babylonian and Jewish blood that settled in what is present day northern Iraq.

"Why, did you have this meeting with this old man?"

"I was like you, looking for gold; I was introduced to him through a fellow business acquaintance."

"I remember now, his name – Ben Tar Abram." Hugo leaned forward to grab his drink and with a broad smile he said again, "That's his name – the old man, Ben Tar Abram."

"How did you remember his name?"

"Simple, *mon cher ami*, I will explain another day." Hugo had not finished explaining what the old man had told him. The old man had said that he believed the Yazidis people practised a religion today, similar to the

Jews and the Christians. But, he believed with several distinct differences that made the Yazidis people unique among the great religions of the world. The old man explained that the Yazidis people believe in one God, but Hugo could not remember what more the old man had to say.

"That's it, that's all I know, *mon cher ami*."

"Thanks, Hugo. The Sheik was right. They are a clue – the Yazidis, it's their religion, there is something about their religion that I believe is the clue."

***

Pharrell had arranged over the phone to meet with Angelique at the Grand Hotel the following day. Angelique had told him that she had some important information that she wanted to share with Pharrell. She had said that it was too important to reveal over the phone to him, and she had said that you never knew who was listening over the phone. Besides, she had said she wanted to see Pharrell before she was assigned another story in another country.

That morning Pharrell was sat outside the Grand Hotel's bar waiting for Angelique to arrive. From where he sat he could observe the melee of people busily trying to cross the roads amongst the morning traffic in the centre of the city. Angelique had said to him, not to bother picking her up from the airport because she had other business to contend with. Instead, he had had time to think. He saw how other couples held hands and he felt the passion within him leap to the surface. He knew what he really wanted now.

In the distance, through the crowd of people trying to get where they were going, he saw the diminutive face of the woman he loved. Before he had time to compose himself, she had already waved and was making her way to his table. With a hug and kiss she said, "I 'm glad you chose to sit outside. What I've got to say is between you and me only."

"I had been wondering for hours what you had to tell me. So, please tell me."

"I'm not who you think I am, I work for the F.B.I. My real name is Sarah Milligan." There was a brief pause before she said, "Does it change anything for you?"

"No, it's only a name, and besides what's in a name?" Pharrell was briefly shocked at the news, but felt the same as before and said, "You're still the same girl I've fallen in love with."

Sarah smiled and said, "I've decided to retire from the F.B.I. and from there I don't have any plans."

Pharrell caught the eye of the waitress and ordered some more drinks, before considering his reply. "Perhaps, we should celebrate and consider our plans for the future?"

"What about that camel ride you promised me, that sounds fun." Sarah said with a cute smile.

Pharrell returned the smile with his own beaming grin and said, "Have you heard about the legend of Queen Hatshepsut and the Temple of 'Splendour of Splendours'?"

****

In the legend of the richest king of Babylon the messenger came and went, and, in the end, history was pointing to a warning sign, Babylon, said the Bible, shall never be rebuilt, and nor shall people or animals dwell there. And, to this day, Babylon is deserted and the treasure remains elusive as ever.

Anthony Fox

www.ingramcontent.com/pod-product-compliance
Lightning Source LLC
Chambersburg PA
CBHW020639220526
45464CB00001B/209